Books are to be returned on or before

Frontispiece The Royal Red Cross, 1914 Star, British War and Victory Medals awarded to Sister Frances Maud Rice TFNS

Army Service Records
of the First World War

Army Service Records
of the First World War

William Spencer

Third expanded edition

PUBLIC RECORD OFFICE

Public Record Office Readers' Guide No. 19

Public Record Office
Kew
Richmond
Surrey TW9 4DU

ISBN 1 903365 23 6

British Library Cataloguing-in-Publication Data
A catalogue record for this book is available from the British Library

Printed by The Cromwell Press Ltd, Trowbridge, Wiltshire

Contents

Illustrations

Foreword

During the last 25 years there has been a renaissance of scholarly interest in the history of the British Army during the Great War. This has largely been made possible by the release of records from the Ministry of Defence to the Public Record Office, beginning in 1968, especially the 10,000 unit War Diaries (WO 95) and their associated 'after action reports' and 'lessons learned'. These records have made possible a fruitful study of the British Army as an institution, free from the increasingly sterile debates about the personal failings of a few leading commanders. This was entirely to the good, but it had the eventual effect – perhaps – of depersonalizing the army, in whose ranks more than 5.7 million men served during the war, a significant proportion of the British male population. This omission began to be repaired with the gradual release of soldiers' personal files – which started on Armistice Day 1996 – and the release of approximately 216,000 officers' personal files, which began in February 1998. The availability of these records now makes it possible to put the individual soldier and officer back at the heart of the British war effort. William Spencer's new edition of *Army Service Records of the First World War* provides an invaluable and significantly revised introduction to the use of these records that offers, for the first time, not only an explanation of the records themselves and how to use them but also how they came to be the way they are, which is to say imperfect from the point of view of the modern researcher. The guide will be warmly welcomed by family, military and social historians with an interest in this most controversial and compelling of conflicts.

Dr J. M. Bourne
Department of Modern History
University of Birmingham

Preface

The origins of this guide can be found in *Army Service Records of the First World War*, by Simon Fowler, Stuart Tamblin and myself. I revised the book for a second edition which was produced in 1998 to coincide with the release of the officers' records of service.

There are number of reasons for this third and completely restructured edition. Since 1998 more records of service concerning nurses, Women's Auxiliary Army Corps and other ranks have been released. The release of First World War records of service of other ranks, both male and female, has continued and should be completed by 2002. Added to these other ranks' records, are a number of very important senior officers' files, including that of Field Marshal Sir Douglas Haig. The only records of service for the First World War period that will not be available, will be those for other ranks that saw further service after 1920, and officers who served on after March 1922.

There are numerous people to thank for providing their help in producing this work: my colleagues in the PRO, Anne Kilminster, Sheila Knight, Guy Grannum, Hugh Alexander, Brian Carter and Paul Johnson; and friends and contacts including Paul Marsden of the Department of Defence in Ottawa, Keith Adams of the British Library Newspaper Library at Colindale, David Lloyd, Paul Baillie, Jim Day, Dave Morris, Tony Farrington and significantly Keith Steward.

I must thank John Bourne for agreeing to write a foreword and Professor Brian Bond for maintaining and increasing my interest in the First World War.

My final thanks as always go to Kate, Lucy and Alice for allowing me to neglect my duties as a husband and father, and to scatter papers all over the house.

Using the PRO

The Public Record Office is the national repository for government records in the UK. Its main site at Kew holds the surviving records of government back to the Domesday Book (1086) and beyond. The records already occupy more than 170 km of shelving and are increasing every day. The PRO at Kew is usually the best place to go to search for an ancestor in the armed forces.

Public Record Office
Kew
Richmond
Surrey TW9 4DU
General telephone: 020 8876 3444
Telephone number for enquiries and advance ordering of documents (with exact references only): 020 8392 5200
Internet: http://www.pro.gov.uk/

Opening times (closed Sundays, public holidays, and for annual stocktaking)

Monday	9 a.m. to 5 p.m.
Tuesday	10 a.m. to 7 p.m.
Wednesday	9 a.m. to 5 p.m.
Thursday	9 a.m. to 7 p.m.
Friday	9 a.m. to 5 p.m.
Saturday	9.30 a.m. to 5 p.m.

Note that the last time for ordering documents is 4 p.m. on Mondays, Wednesdays and Fridays; 4.30 p.m. on Tuesdays and Thursdays, and 2.30 p.m. on Saturdays.

The PRO is about ten minutes' walk from Kew Gardens Underground Station, which is on London Transport's District Line, as well as the North London Line Silverlink Metro service. For motorists it is just off the South Circular Road (A205). There is adequate parking, as well as a public restaurant, bookshop, self-service lockers, extensive library, and Education and Visitor Centre.

The PRO can be a confusing place on your first visit, but staff are knowledgable and friendly and happy to help. No appointment is needed to visit, but you will need a reader's ticket to gain access to research areas. To obtain a ticket take with you a full UK driving licence or UK banker's card, or a passport if you are a British citizen, and your passport or national identity card if you are not a British citizen.

To protect the documents, each one of which is unique, security in the reading rooms is tight. You are only permitted to take a notebook and notes (up to six loose sheets) into the reading rooms, where eating, drinking and smoking are not permitted.

The PRO 'On-line'

As well as giving information on where the PRO is, opening times and how to gain access, the PRO website gives details about popular records, including leaflets and lists of researchers. Most importantly the website allows readers to access the PRO catalogue (series lists). The catalogue, PROCAT, can be searched by using keywords, and if you know them, the department code and series.

The men and women of the First World War and their records

1.1 How many?

A two-part question which is frequently asked by researchers looking for something about an individual who served in some capacity is 'How many people served in the First World War and how many records does the PRO hold?'

The answer to the first part of this question is that over 8 million men and women saw service in the British forces between 1914 and 1918. At the outbreak of war the Army numbered 733,514 men and by the end of the war 7,712,772 men and women had enlisted. The Royal Flying Corps (RFC) numbered only 1,900 men but by the end of the war 293,522 had enlisted in the RFC and RAF (Royal Air Force). The total naval enlistments numbered some 407,360. The total number of men and women who enlisted and saw service in the British armed forces between 1914 and 1918 was 9,296,691.

The number of enlistments during the war can be found in *Statistics of Military Effort of the British Empire during the Great War* (1922), however, to place the records and the men and women who can be found in them into some sort of perspective, it is worth noting the following:

Strength of British Army, Territorials and Reserves as at August 1914   733,514
Enlistments August 1914–December 1915   2,466,719

Without adding the remaining enlistments for the rest of the war to these figures, this number has already exceeded the total number of records of service held in WO 339, WO 363, WO 364 and WO 374.

The second part of the question is a little more difficult to answer. Whilst the records discussed in this guide certainly number in the millions, an accurate total of surviving First World War records may never be known. There are a number of reasons for this uncertainty.

The most significant reason for this uncertainty is the Arnside Street fire on 8 September 1940. Arnside Street was the location of the War Office records repository and in it were housed various records of those personnel who had seen service in the

First World War. The majority of the records housed in the repository were either totally destroyed or badly damaged by fire and water. All that survived the fire are being preserved at the PRO.

The second reason for the uncertainty is duplication. Although there are some 16 series containing records of service of the First World War period, many men and women had service files held by more than one government department and many of these duplicates have been preserved either in a WO record series or a PIN record series.

From the 7 million plus enlistments for all services must be taken the records of those who saw any service after 1920 as an other rank, or after March 1922 as an officer. This includes those whose service ended within the above prescribed dates but who were recalled or re-enlisted for service in the Second World War. These records are still maintained by the Ministry of Defence.

1.2 Why the records are the way that they are

Information regarding the physical structure and state of the officers' records are discussed elsewhere (see **Chapter 2**). As a greater percentage of surviving records are for officers, you are more likely to find a record for an officer than for an other rank. However, it is the records of the other ranks that generate the most interest and the most questions.

No-one knows how the War Office record repository on Arnside Street was laid out. Therefore, until a complete survey of the surviving soldiers' records is completed, which units' personnel records are there and which are not, will remain subject to speculation.

At the end of the Second World War in order to supplement the surviving records and to replace those lost in 1940, the War Office made an appeal to those other government departments that might have held records of service type material, to return them to the War Office. The Ministry of Pensions returned the largest collection, relating to men who had been discharged from the army suffering from either wounds or sickness. These records are in WO 364. The arrangement of all of the records at that time is unknown. However, all of the surviving records were put into alphabetical sequences after the Second World War. The 'Burnt' records are in WO 363 and the 'Unburnt' records, already mentioned, are in WO 364.

The surviving other ranks' records of service are held in some 44,000 boxes. As the collection is so big and the majority of it is too delicate to be handled, with the help of the Heritage Lottery Fund, the records are being made available on microfilm. By the time the project is finished in the summer of 2002, over 15,000 reels of microfilm will have been produced. On these films will be preserved the military careers of some 2.8 million individuals. Added to the 217,000 officers' files this will mean that some 3 million records which document individuals of the First World War will be available for all to see.

This guide is to help those people who have an interest in the men and women of the First World War to find out something about them, when they served, where they served, where they fought and died, where they are buried or commemorated, what medals they were awarded, and much more.

2 Officers' records of service

2.1 Introduction

Prior to the outbreak of the First World War, there were approximately 15,000 officers holding commissions. During the period of hostilities another 235,000 individuals were granted either temporary or permanent commissions in the British Army.

From a total of some 250,000 officers who held a commission at any time between 1914 and 1918, the records of some individuals are not available. Officers who were still serving after 31 March 1922 or who had left the army prior to that date but **rejoined or were recalled** for further service, for example in the Second World War, have files still retained by the Ministry of Defence. In most cases the files retained can be identified by the presence of a 'P' number file reference alongside the officers' names in WO 338. The 'P' file system replaced all of the other officers' file references which had been used during the war. This new file system started on 1 April 1922 and apart from the exceptional cases where files may be found, for example in WO 138 (see section **2.6.4**), all of the 'P' files are with the Ministry of Defence.

The two main record series containing records of service of officers who saw service in the First World War represent the careers of some 217,000 individuals. Amongst these files can be found many well known names, some famous for their service during the war, others for something they did before or after the war. It is unfair to name specific people as I believe all of those whose service is represented by these records are as equally important as the Kings, Emperors, soldiers, statesmen, poets and murderers. They are there for you to discover.

Originally an officer's file consisted of three main parts; the record of service in the form of the Army Form B 199 (AF B 199), the confidential reports in the Army Form B 196 and the correspondence file. In all but the rarest of cases, only the correspondence file has survived.

The AF B 199 was a single sheet, completed on both sides, which contained most of the relevant data about an officer, including his biographical details, qualifications, courses he had attended, details about active service and any awards he received. The information on the forms was entered as events occurred. As they would appear rather untidy with lots of different styles of writing on them, the forms were renewed every five years, the entries being completed in one colour of ink, in one hand.

The reason for the lack of at least two parts of most officers' records of service can be explained. The AF 199s for officers commissioned prior to 1901 may be found bound in Army Book 83s in WO 76. The confidential reports for officers of the same period no longer survive. The correspondence files for these men, in most cases do not survive unless they were recalled for service during the First World War, having retired prior to 1914, or were still serving when war broke out. Even then in many cases files no longer exist.

The AF B 199s and AF B 196s for officers who were commissioned after 1901, were separated from the correspondence files and stored at the Arnside Street record repository, where they were destroyed in 1940. In between the extraction of these parts of the whole files, the remaining correspondence in each file underwent the usual record keeping practice of being weeded of all unimportant material. It must be remembered that the War Office still had access to the two parts of the file it had removed and therefore only kept that type of information which was not kept on an AF B 199 or AF B 196. The consequence of standard archival practice and the destruction of the more informative parts of most officers' files in 1940, is that all that survives may seem very bland and uninformative but there is a reason for it. What remains relates primarily to money, length of service, pensions for wounds and the settling of deceased officers' estates.

Unlike the records of service of other ranks where there can usually be found a collection of standard Army Forms, in the case of officers' files, the physical contents of the files vary more greatly. Depending upon the circumstances of the route to a commission, so the types of Army Forms vary. The files of those officers commissioned from the ranks usually contain the other ranks' records of service and their Army Form B 103 Casualty Form – Active service. Initial forms relating to commissions come in four main types (shown in **Figs 1–4**):

- Army Form B 201. Application for Appointment to the Special Reserve of Officers
- Army Form MT 939. Application for Appointment to a Temporary Commission in the Regular Army for the Period of the War
- Army Form W 3361. Notification of Posting on First Appointment
- For Officers commissioned prior to August 1914. A Form of Particulars: Examination for Admission to the Royal Military Academy (Sandhurst) or Royal Military College (Woolwich)

2.2 Types of commissions

During the First World War there were different types of commission depending on the status of the unit in which a man served or the preference of the individual being commissioned.

Those officers who were holding commissions prior to the outbreak of the war held either permanent commissions in the Regular Army, territorial commissions or commissions in the reserve of officers. The officers who were holding Territorial Army commissions at the outbreak of the war could originally have held a commission in the Militia, Special Reserve, Yeomanry or Volunteers. These commissions are in parts of the army that were united into the Territorial Army upon its creation in 1907.

Officers commissioned during the war were usually granted temporary commissions, in either the Regular Army, the Territorial Army or the Special Reserve of Officers. A small number of officers were granted permanent commissions in the Regular Army.

In most cases it is possible to tell what type of commission had been granted to an officer by consulting the *Army List*. In the name index of the *Army List* letters are used to signify the part of the army into which an officer had been commissioned:

M   Militia
R   Special Reserve of Officers
T   Territorial Force
V   Volunteers
Y   Yeomanry

If there is no prefix alongside the name of an officer then he was commissioned into the Regular Army.

For more information on the *Army List* see section **2.7**.

2.3 WO 338

WO 338 is the name index for the records preserved in WO 339 (see section **2.3.1**) and provides the all important 'Long Number' which needs to be obtained in order that the file can be identified in WO 339. The indexes in WO 338 consist of 24 pieces, all of which are available on microfilm. WO 338/1–21 is the name index for officers commissioned between 1901 and 1922. WO 338/22 is the index of officers commissioned between 1870 and 1901. WO 338/23 is the index of officers of the Royal Army Medical Corps (RAMC) commissioned between 1871 and 1922 but does not include the temporary officers mentioned below in section 2.5.

Army Form B. 201.
(Modified for use during Mobilization).

APPLICATION FOR APPOINTMENT TO THE SPECIAL RESERVE OF OFFICERS.

The candidate will carefully complete the following particulars, obtain the certificates on page 3 and then

If desirous of appointment to

A Household Cavalry Regiment
The Foot Guards
The Irish Horse
King Edward's Horse

A Cavalry Regiment

A reserve unit of the Royal Garrison Artillery
A reserve unit of the Royal Engineers (see note (b) on p. 2)
A reserve unit of Infantry
The Royal Field Artillery

The Royal Garrison Artillery, but not to a reserve unit

The Royal Engineers, but not to a reserve unit

An Infantry Regiment, but not to a reserve unit

The Royal Flying Corps
The Army Service Corps
The Royal Army Medical Corps
The Army Veterinary Corps

Present himself in person to

The Officer Commanding the Regiment he wishes to join

The Officer Commanding a Reserve Regiment of Cavalry, a Cavalry Depot, or the Officer in charge of Cavalry Records, Canterbury

The Officer Commanding the Reserve unit he wishes to join

The Officer Commanding a Reserve Brigade or Depot

The Lieut.-Colonel, Royal Garrison Artillery, in any Coast Defences, or the Officer Commanding a Depot

The President of the Institution of Civil Engineers, Gt. George Street, Westminster, London, S.W., (unless the applicant be a member of the Senior Division of the Officers Training Corps, in which case the application will be forwarded direct to the War Office by the Adjutant of his Contingent.)

The Officer Commanding a Regular battalion or Depot of the Regiment he wishes to join

Forward the application to—The War Office, London, S.W.

NOTED ON CARDS
4. 5. 15.
M. T. 2.

1. Unit or branch in which the candidate desires to serve	3rd Battalion. Royal Welsh Fusiliers.
2. Name of Candidate (in full) Surname ... (*See note (a) on page 2*) Christian Names...	Sassoon Siegfried Lorraine
3. Date of birth (A birth certificate or a baptismal certificate containing the date of birth to be attached or forwarded later.)	Sept. 8th 1886
4. Whether married	No
5. Whether of pure European descent	Yes
6. Whether a British born or a naturalized British subject	British Born.
7. Whether the candidate has:—	
(a) Obtained a leaving or qualifying certificate as required of a candidate for admission to the Royal Military College under the regulations in force up to 1st April, 1912. (Certificate to be attached).	No
(b) Qualified at an Army Entrance Examination. (State date of examination).	no
(c) Passed the matriculation examination of a university, or a test accepted in lieu thereof. (Certificate to be attached.)	Yes.
Or failing one of the above:—	
(d) Can produce a statement from the headmaster of a secondary school, or other competent educational authority, as to his educational attainments. (Statement to be attached.)	
8. Permanent address	Weirleigh. Paddock Wood. Kent
9. Present address for correspondence	Weirleigh
10. Profession or occupation	none.
11. Schools and Colleges at which educated	Marlborough College.
12. Whether now serving, or previously served, in any branch of His Majesty's Naval or Military Forces. If so, state :—	
(a) Regiment or Corps ...	Sussex Yeomanry.
(b) Date of appointment ...	4th August. 1914
(c) Rank ...	Private.
(d) Date of retirement, resignation or discharge	Still serving
(e) Circumstances of retirement, resignation or discharge (A Candidate who has served in the ranks should attach his discharge certificate).	

(8 8 10) 5000 8/14 H W V Forms B 201
5000 9/14

[P.T.O.

Figure 1 Appointment of Siegfried Sassoon to the Special Reserve of Officers. Army Form B 201 (WO 339/51440)

List of WO 338 Indexes

WO 338	Date range	Surnames
1	1901–22	A
2	1901–22	Ba–Bl
3	1901–22	Bo–By
4	1901–22	Ca–Cl
5	1901–22	Co–Cz
6	1901–22	D
7	1901–22	E–F
8	1901–22	G
9	1901–22	Ha–Hep
10	1901–22	Her–Hy
11	1901–22	I–K
12	1901–22	L
13	1901–22	Ma–Michaelson
14	1901–22	Micholson–O
15	1901–22	P
16	1901–22	Q–R
17	1901–22	Sa–Smith, George
18	1901–22	Smith, Gerald–Sz
19	1901–22	T–V
20	1901–22	Wa–Wilber
21	1901–22	Wilberforce–Z
22	1870–1901	Old Numbers A–Z
23	1871–1921	Medical Officers A–Z

The format of WO 338 is common to all pieces and the information is presented in six columns:

Surname   Initial(s)   Regt/Corps   Long Number   Rank   Remarks

Most of the information presented in the index is quite obvious. However, although the abbreviations used to denote the corps in which the officer was commissioned can easily be translated, the numerical codes used to identify infantry regiments are those used to identify the regiments prior to the 1881 Cardwell reforms. After 1881 regiments were known by name and not by their old numbers. The original numerical identity of infantry regiments can be found in section **9.7**. If the reference in the 'Long Number' column is made up of letters and numbers, usually the first letter of the surname and the first vowel of the surname, then this is a 'Vowel' reference. Files with 'Vowel' references are usually to be found in WO 374.

138763
1

Form M.T. / M. 393

NOTED ON CARDS
M.T. 1|6|16

This Form is to be used for any candidate who is serving in the ranks of the New Armies, Special Reserve, or Territorial Force, and for any other candidate who is neither a cadet or ex-cadet of the Senior Division, Officers Training Corps, nor a member of a University.

Form M.T./392 should be used for an Officers Training Corps (Senior Division) or University candidate, who is not serving in the ranks.

APPLICATION FOR APPOINTMENT TO A TEMPORARY COMMISSION IN THE REGULAR ARMY FOR THE PERIOD OF THE WAR.

The candidate will complete the following particulars and obtain certificates below as to character and educational qualification.

1. Name in full { Surname. / Christian names.	Griffin. / William Harold.
2. Date and place of birth.	1st October 1884. Salford. Lancs.
3. Whether married.	Widower (no family)
4. Whether of pure European descent.	Yes! ✓
5. Whether a British subject by birth or naturalization. (State which, and if by naturalization attach a certificate from the Home Office.)	British Birth.
6. Nationality by birth of father (if naturalized, state date.)	British
7. Occupation of father.	Manager. (Engineering Works)
8. Permanent address of candidate.	103 West High St. Salford. Lancs.
9. Present address for correspondence.	19th (S) Royal Fusiliers.
10. School or Schools at which educated.	Salford Technical School.
11. Occupation or employment in civil life.	Municipal Accountant.
12. Whether able to ride.	Yes!
13. Whether now serving, or previously served, in any branch of His Majesty's Naval or Military Forces, or in the Officers Training Corps. If so, state:—	
(a) Regiment, Corps, or Contingent	19th (S) R.F.
(b) Date of appointment	1st May 1915
(c) If serving in the ranks state whether on an ordinary peace engagement or for the period of the war only	Period War.
(d) Rank	Private (Signaller).
(e) Date of retirement, resignation or discharge	—
(f) Circumstances of retirement, resignation or discharge	— ✓
14. Whether now serving, or previously served, in any other Government Department (Home, Indian, or Colonial). If so, give particulars.	No!
15. Whether an application for a commission has been previously made, if so, on what date and for what branch of the service.	No!

(7 30 32) G. D. 6684/2 20,000 11/15 H W V(P 560)   H. 15/1275
W 16351—5516 20,000 1/16

Figure 2 Application for Appointment to a Temporary Commission for Lt W. Griffin. Army Form MT 939 (WO 339/63641)

WO 338 example

The index entry for the poet Siegfried Sassoon who saw service in the Royal Welch Fusiliers (originally the 23rd Foot) will be found in WO 338/17 Sa–Smith, George, and will be displayed thus:

Surname	Initial(s)	Regt/Corps	Long Number	Rank
Sassoon	S. L.	23	122091	2 Lt

To convert this into the correct file in WO 339, see section **2.3.1**.

2.3.1 WO 339

The files preserved in WO 339 comprise the records of 139,906 officers who saw service during the First World War. The majority of the files are for officers who were duration of the war officers: 'Temporary Gentlemen' only. It is in this series that most of the officers who held Regular Army commissions and who were still serving at the outbreak of the war can be found, together with those granted emergency commissions in the Regular Army and those granted commissions in the Special Reserve of Officers. At the end of the WO 339 record series are a number of files for British Army other ranks who were commissioned into the Indian Army. See **Chapter 5** for further information.

WO 338 to WO 339 conversion example

In order to find a file in WO 339, it is necessary to locate an officer's 'Long Number' and then convert it into a WO 339 document reference.

Siegfried Sassoon had the 'Long Number' 122091, as located in WO 338/17 (see section **2.3** above). In the WO 339 catalogue the 'Long Number' or former reference, is in the right hand column and the PRO WO 339 reference is in the left hand column. Thus by tracing the 'Long Number' in the right hand column the reference for Siegfried Sassoon's file (WO 339/51440) can be found.

WO 339 catalogue

Column headings

PRO department and series	Surname and initial(s)	Long Number
WO 339 51440	Sassoon S L	122091

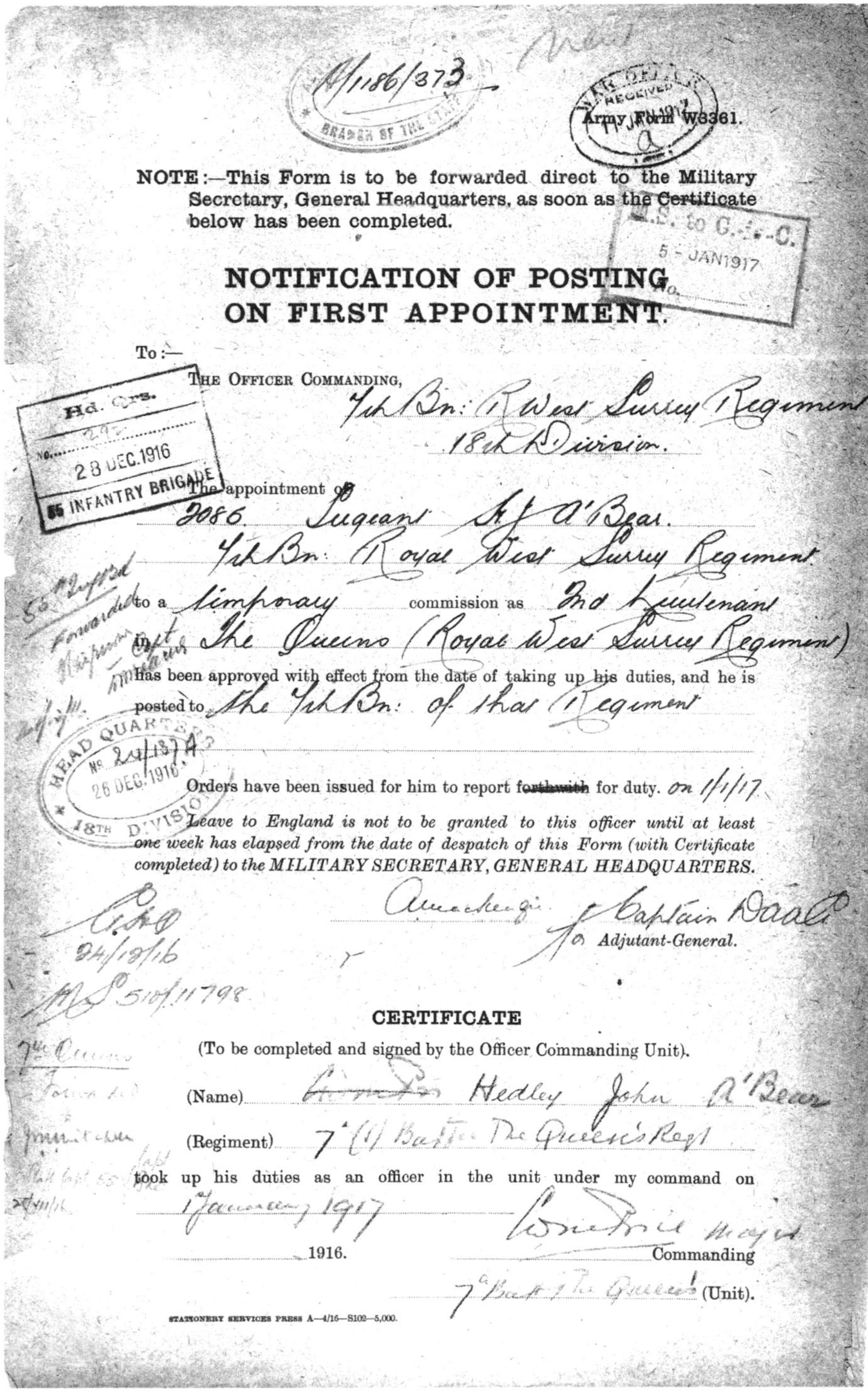

M/1186/373

Army Form W3361.

NOTE:—This Form is to be forwarded direct to the Military Secretary, General Headquarters, as soon as the Certificate below has been completed.

M.S. to G.H.-C. 5 - JAN 1917

NOTIFICATION OF POSTING ON FIRST APPOINTMENT.

To:—

The Officer Commanding, 7th Bn: R West Surrey Regiment 18th Division.

Hd. Qrs. 28 DEC. 1916 55 INFANTRY BRIGADE

The appointment of 2086 Sergeant H J A'Bear. 7th Bn: Royal West Surrey Regiment

to a temporary commission as 2nd Lieutenant in The Queens (Royal West Surrey Regiment) has been approved with effect from the date of taking up his duties, and he is posted to the 7th Bn: of that Regiment

HEAD QUARTERS No 24/1874 26 DEC. 1916 18TH DIVISION

Orders have been issued for him to report ~~forthwith~~ for duty. on 1/1/17

Leave to England is not to be granted to this officer until at least one week has elapsed from the date of despatch of this Form (with Certificate completed) to the MILITARY SECRETARY, GENERAL HEADQUARTERS.

Captain for Adjutant-General.

24/12/16

MS 510/11798

CERTIFICATE

(To be completed and signed by the Officer Commanding Unit).

(Name) Hedley John A'Bear

(Regiment) 7th (S) Battn The Queen's Regt

took up his duties as an officer in the unit under my command on 1 January 1917

1916. Major Commanding

7th Batt. The Queen's (Unit).

STATIONERY SERVICES PRESS A—4/16—S102—5,000.

Figure 3 Notification of Posting on First Appointment of 2/Lt H. J. A'Bear. Army Form W 3361 (WO 339/117622)

What must be remembered when using WO 339 is that the content of the files is mostly correspondence relating to an officer and his service, rather than a record of service.

2.4 WO 374

The files preserved in WO 374, consist of the files of officers of the Territorial Army, a number of officers who came out of retirement, and other officers who do not really fit either the Regular or Territorial Army; the civilian specialists who were granted commissions on account of certain skills which the army needed.

Unlike WO 339 which is arranged by 'Long Number', WO 374 is arranged in alphabetical order, which includes all initials and rank (usually the highest confirmed rank an officer held).

2.5 Royal Army Medical Corps (temporary) commissions

During the First World War a large number of men with medical training were needed to cope with the high numbers of casualties. As a result of this need many doctors were granted temporary commissions in the Royal Army Medical Corps. As these officers were a discrete group, they were given their own series of records of service; the 24 Series. Unfortunately, as these RAMC (Temp) officers were only needed for the war, their records were all destroyed after 1920. Amongst these temporary officers whose records no longer exist are perhaps two of the most important doctors of the war: Noel Chavasse, VC and bar, MC, and James Churchill Dunn, DSO, MC, DCM, author of *The War the Infantry Knew*.

For an in depth study of doctors in war, the problems relating to recruitment and the increasing need for more doctors due to the number of casualties and the diverse range of injuries, *Doctors in the Great War* by Ian R. Whitehead (1999), is the best book.

2.6 Other record series

There are a number of other record series that contain officers' records of service.

2.6.1 WO 25

In WO 25 there is a small collection of Royal Engineers officers' records and they are arranged by initial commission date. Although most of the volumes are pre-First

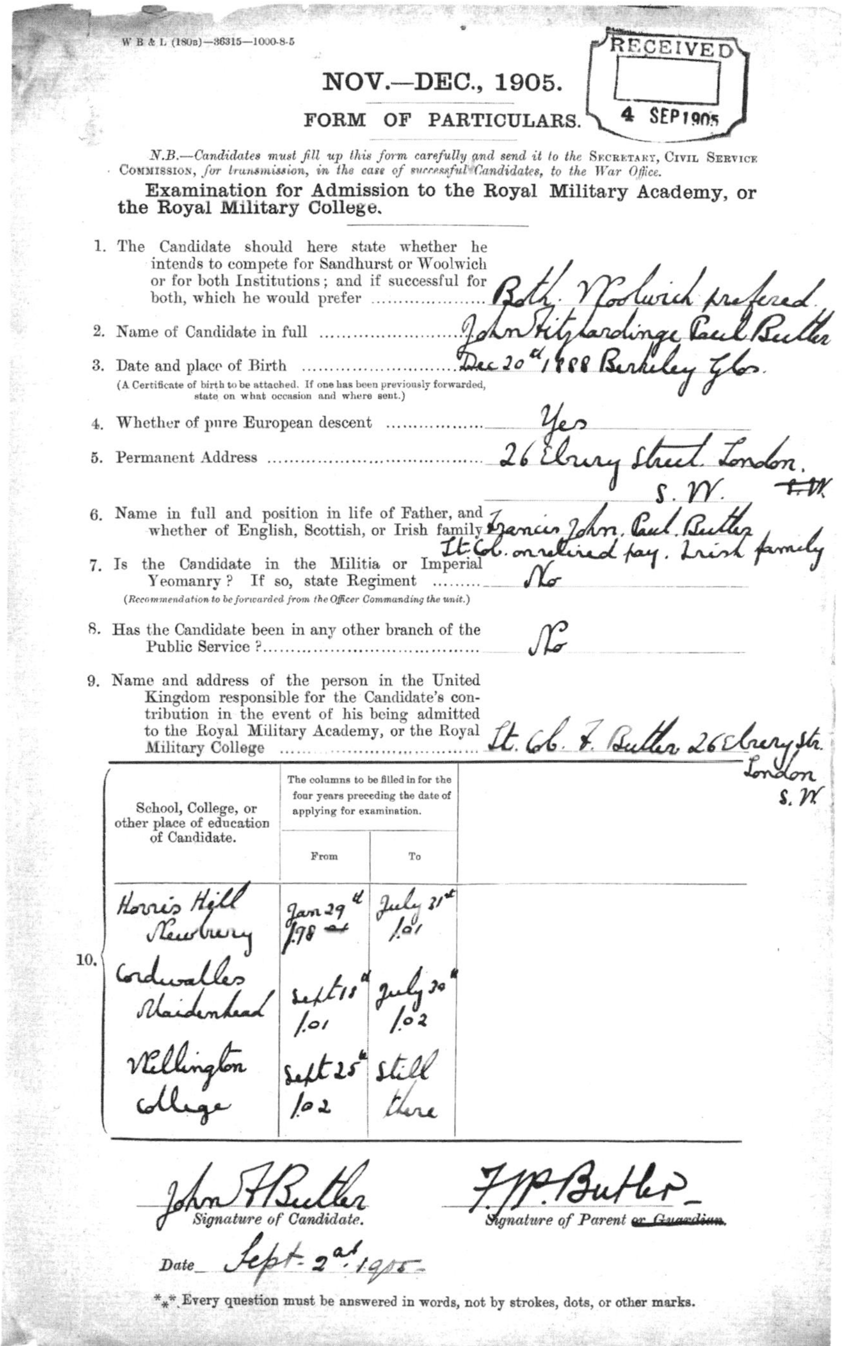

W B & L (180a)—36315—1000-8-5

RECEIVED
4 SEP 1905

NOV.—DEC., 1905.

FORM OF PARTICULARS.

N.B.—Candidates must fill up this form carefully and send it to the SECRETARY, CIVIL SERVICE COMMISSION, *for transmission, in the case of successful Candidates, to the War Office.*

Examination for Admission to the Royal Military Academy, or the Royal Military College.

1. The Candidate should here state whether he intends to compete for Sandhurst or Woolwich or for both Institutions; and if successful for both, which he would prefer .... Both. Woolwich prefered.
2. Name of Candidate in full .... John Fitzhardinge Paul Butler
3. Date and place of Birth .... Dec 20th 1888 Berkeley Glos.
   (A Certificate of birth to be attached. If one has been previously forwarded, state on what occasion and where sent.)
4. Whether of pure European descent .... Yes
5. Permanent Address .... 26 Ebury Street London. S.W.
6. Name in full and position in life of Father, and whether of English, Scottish, or Irish family Francis John Paul Butler Lt Col. on retired pay. Irish family
7. Is the Candidate in the Militia or Imperial Yeomanry? If so, state Regiment .... No
   (*Recommendation to be forwarded from the Officer Commanding the unit.*)
8. Has the Candidate been in any other branch of the Public Service ?.................................... No
9. Name and address of the person in the United Kingdom responsible for the Candidate's contribution in the event of his being admitted to the Royal Military Academy, or the Royal Military College .... Lt Col. F. Butler 26 Ebury Str. London S.W.

10.

School, College, or other place of education of Candidate.	The columns to be filled in for the four years preceding the date of applying for examination. From	To
Horris Hill Newbury	Jan 29th /98	July 31st /01
Cordwalles Maidenhead	Sept 11th /01	July 30th /02
Wellington College	Sept 25th /02	still there

John F. Butler
Signature of Candidate.

F. P. Butler
Signature of Parent ~~or Guardian~~.

Date Sept. 2nd 1905

*** Every question must be answered in words, not by strokes, dots, or other marks.

Figure 4 Form of Particulars: Examination for Admission to the Royal Military Academy (Sandhurst) or Royal Military College (Woolwich) for J. F. P. Butler VC, DSO (WO 339/6730)

World War, they do contain those pre-war officers and a number commissioned from the ranks in the early years of the war:

Reference	Date
WO 25/3913	1796–1860
WO 25/3914	1860–1921
WO 25/3915	1873–1928
WO 25/3916	1886–1918
WO 25/3917	1885–1937
WO 25/3918	1895–1935
WO 25/3919	1904–15
WO 25/3920	1879–1915 includes Supplementary Reserve

2.6.2 WO 76

The surviving records of service for officers of the infantry and the cavalry, together with the Royal Engineers (Militia) officers, can be found in WO 76. These records date from the early nineteenth century to the First World War period and are arranged by record office and then by unit whose records were held by the particular record office.

The collection in WO 76 is, however, very inconsistent in both the date coverage and the units the record series covers. Whilst the complete series of records for the 1st battalion of a regiment may be found in WO 76, it is possible that the 2nd battalion may be missing, either in part or in total.

Records of the 3rd and 4th battalions of infantry regiments may also be found in WO 76.

2.6.3 WO 68

The records preserved in WO 68 consist of various types relating to the Militia. Arranged by unit, the records in this series include officers' records of service, bounty books for payments to other ranks, and records of units' services. Many of the records in WO 68 run up to the immediate pre-war period. Some include the period 1914–18. Further details about these records can be found in *Records of the Militia and Volunteer Forces 1757–1945* by William Spencer (1998).

2.6.4 WO 138

The records of service preserved in the record series WO 138 may not be many but they are a very significant collection of officers' files covering the nineteenth and twentieth centuries. Amongst the files in this record series are a number of very important files belonging to officers who saw service in the First World War. Most of these files concern officers whose service led to an official War Office enquiry into their actions. The files of a number of officers who were sacked from an appointment during the war are preserved here, and the files not only contain their basic records of service but also detailed correspondence concerning their conduct which resulted in them being dismissed.

WO 138/75–77 contains the surviving records of Field Marshal Sir Douglas Haig. Whilst the amount of papers in these three files is impressive, they are primarily concerned with Haig's retired pay, his funeral in 1928, and the construction of a statue of him.

Other individuals whose files are in WO 138 include the poet Wilfred Owen and a number of significant generals of the war including E. J. M. Stuart-Wortley, commander of 46 Division on 1 July 1916, and Brigadier General A. E. Aitken, commander of the forces that attempted to land at Tanga in German East Africa in 1914.

2.6.5 The Royal Flying Corps and Royal Air Force (RFC and RAF)

For a full explanation of the records of the RFC and RAF see *Air Force Records for Family Historians* by William Spencer (2000), and also Chapter 6.

In most cases officers of the RFC were commissioned into another unit before transferring into the RFC. Records of service of RFC officers can be found in WO 339 and WO 374 and can be found by using the methods described in sections **2.3**, **2.3.1** and **2.4**. In the Regt/Corps column of WO 338 (see section **2.3**), RFC may be found either alongside the original unit designation, or it may have replaced the original unit identity.

The other record series which contains RFC/RAF officers' records of service is AIR 76, which is available on microfilm. AIR 76 is arranged in alphabetical order by surname and contains the records of those officers who had left the RAF by early 1920. Interestingly AIR 76 contains information about a number of officers of the RFC who were killed before the RAF was formed in April 1918.

2.6.6 The Royal Naval Division (RND)

The Royal Naval Division was formed in 1914 from some 30,000 surplus sailors for whom the Royal Navy had no ships. The RND saw service at Antwerp in 1914 and in Gallipoli in 1915, before returning to France in 1916.

Prior to 1916 the RND had been under Admiralty control and the division was manned by sailors and royal marines. In 1916 the RND was transferred to War Office control and was renamed 63rd (RN) Division. With the transfer to War Office control the division finally acquired its own artillery and other supporting arms. Whilst most of the infantry were sailors and marines, the artillery and other support personnel were soldiers.

A collection of records of service of the Royal Naval Division can be found in ADM 339. This record series, which is available on microfiche, is split into three distinct parts: other ranks; officers; and those members of the division who were discharged dead. All three sections are arranged in alphabetical order by surname.

As is usual with many records of service, the records in ADM 339 can provide basic biographical data, date of enlistment, information about leave, wounds, honours and awards, and also the name and address of the next of kin.

In most cases, records of service for officers of the RND can also be found in WO 339. When using the WO 338 index, RND will be found in the unit column. In many cases officers of the RND were RNVR officers, and their records can be found in ADM 337. Military Information Leaflet 71, 'The Royal Naval Volunteer Reserve, 1903–1919' provides data about the records in ADM 337.

2.7 The *Army List*

The *Army List* was, and still is, the official listing of all those officers holding a commission in the British Army. There was also an *Indian Army List*. The prime purpose of the *Army List* is to list the names of officers, giving the dates of their commissions and the unit they are serving in.

Copies of the *Army List* are available on the open shelves in the PRO Microfilm Reading Room and Library at Kew. Copies of the *Indian Army List* are available in the PRO Library.

During the First World War period there were a number of different *Army Lists* whose contents varied according to when they were published. The most frequently published list was the monthly *Army List* which listed *all* officers whether they were Regular Army, Territorial Army, or reserve of army officers, giving their commission dates in the ranks they held at the time the list was published and the units they were serving in.

By using the monthly *Army Lists* it is possible to follow the promotions of an officer, and to see which unit(s) he served in.

The quarterly and half yearly *Army Lists* contain information only on officers holding permanent commissions. These lists are arranged by rank and then in graduation order, i.e. the date upon which an officer was promoted to a given rank. By using these lists it is possible to find information such as date of birth, date of first and subsequent commissions, staff appointments, courses the officer has attended and brief details concerning war service. The War Services section of these lists, published in January, provide information about the campaigns the officers were involved in and any medals they were awarded for those campaigns. The quarterly *Army Lists* were published in January, April, July and October.

There is a name index in the back of each *Army List* which refers you to a given column or page number within the main body of the *List*.

Army Lists can be used to see how the Army listed officers' surnames. This is especially important if the officer had a hyphenated surname as the arrangement of the name may help you to find an officer in the Medal Index Cards.

The monthly *Army Lists* include the units and officers of the Dominion forces which served as part of the British Army.

A typical page from a monthly *Army List* can be seen in **Fig 5**.

2.8 Other printed lists

There are a number of other printed lists concerning officers which are available at the PRO. Some of these lists concern officers who died during the war and they are mentioned in the appropriate chapter. Many regimental histories, some of which are available in the PRO Library, contain lists of officers. *A List of Commissioned Medical Officers of The Army 1660–1960* lists members of the Regular Army who were commissioned into the RAMC. A list of the Regular Army members of the Durham Light Infantry can be found in *Officers of the Durham Light Infantry Vol 1 (Regulars)* by Malcolm McGregor (1989) available in the PRO Library.

Senior officers and War Office civil servants, many of whom were former army officers, can be found in the *War Office List*, copies of which can be found in the Microfilm Reading Room.

2.9 Disability pension files PIN 26

A small number of disability pension files maintained by the Ministry of Pensions can be found in PIN 26/19924–19954 and 21066–22756. Arranged in alphabetical order,

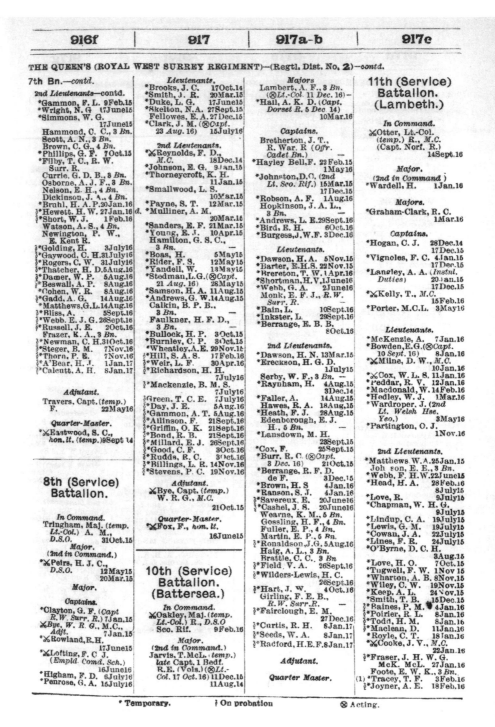

Figure 5 A typical entry in monthly *Army List*, this being the first entry for 2/Lt H. J. A'Bear (*Army List*, March 1917)

these files contain brief information about the individuals' service and more about their medical histories and the payment of the pensions they were awarded.

2.10 The King's African Rifles and West African Frontier Force

Many officers of the British Army saw service in the King's African Rifles (KAR) or in the West African Frontier Force (WAFF) in either the Gold Coast Regiment, Nigeria Regiment or Sierra Leone Battalion. Such attachments are listed in the *Army List*, where relevant sections for these African units can be found.

Correspondence of the KAR and WAFF can be found in CO 534 and CO 445 respectively.

2.11 Case study

Due to the sheer number of officers' files preserved in WO 138, WO 339 and WO 374 it is impossible to describe examples of them all. There are many records common to all officers and many, of course, which are unique. The stimulus for researching the career of an officer of the First World War can come from a number of different sources. What now follows is just one example.

Hedley John A'Bear was born at Waltham St Lawrence in Berkshire in 1893. Along with many young men he was a volunteer and he joined the Army on 2 September 1914 by enlisting into the Queens' Royal West Surrey Regiment at Guildford. Given the service number G2085 Private A'Bear was described as 5 feet 7¼ inches tall, with a fresh complexion, brown eyes and dark brown hair. With numerous other recruits Hedley joined the newly formed 7th Battalion Queen's Royal West Surrey Regiment and along with the remainder of the unit went overseas on 27 July 1915. The battalion was part of the 55th Brigade, 18 (Eastern) Division.

Private A'Bear must have been a good soldier for he was promoted to the rank of corporal on 19 October 1915. Although not recorded in his record of service, he must have been granted a period of leave for on 1 January 1916 he married Winifred Mary Mason at Dunsfold in Surrey.

After he had returned to France the 7th Battalion Queen's Royal West Surrey Regiment were involved in the attack on Montauban on 1 July 1916, the first day of the battle of the Somme. The battalion suffered some 532 casualties and on 8 July Corporal A' Bear was promoted to sergeant. For his service on the Somme Sergeant A'Bear was awarded the Military Medal, which was announced in the *London Gazette* on 6 January 1917.

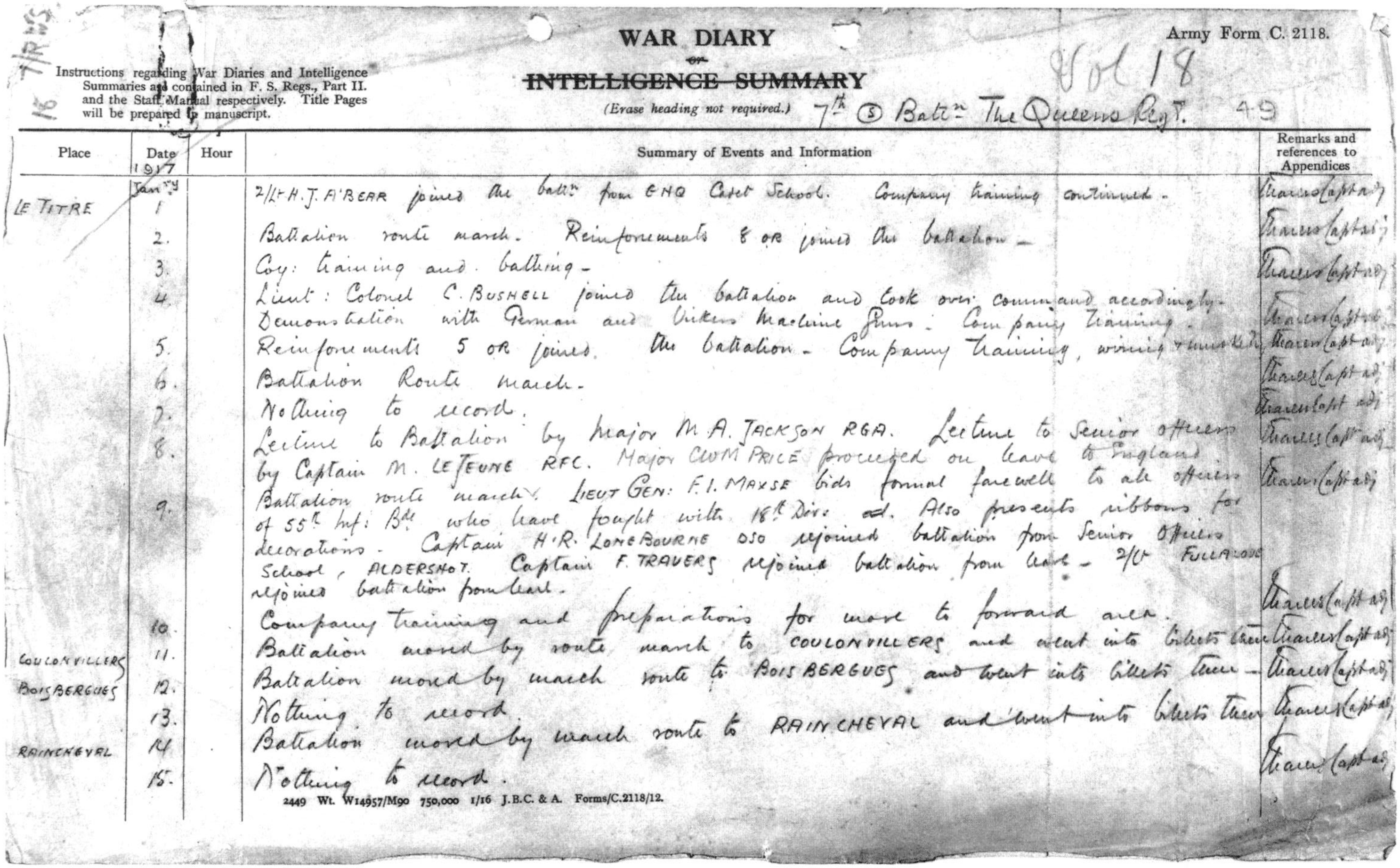

Instructions regarding War Diaries and Intelligence Summaries are contained in F. S. Regs., Part II. and the Staff Manual respectively. Title Pages will be prepared in manuscript.

WAR DIARY
~~or~~
~~**INTELLIGENCE SUMMARY**~~
(Erase heading not required.) 7th (S) Battn: The Queens Regt.

Army Form C. 2118.

Vol 18

49

Place	Date 1917	Hour	Summary of Events and Information	Remarks and references to Appendices
LE TITRE	Jan'y 1		2/Lt H. J. A'BEAR joined the battn from GHQ Cadet School. Company training continued.	Travers (Capt & adj)
	2.		Battalion route march. Reinforcements 8 OR joined the battalion.	Travers (Capt & adj)
	3.		Coy: training and bathing.	Travers (Capt & adj)
	4.		Lieut: Colonel C. BUSHELL joined the battalion and took over command accordingly. Demonstration with German and Vickers Machine Guns. Company training.	Travers (Capt & adj)
	5.		Reinforcements 5 OR joined the battalion. Company training, wiring & musketry.	Travers (Capt & adj)
	6.		Battalion Route march.	Travers (Capt & adj)
	7.		Nothing to record.	Travers (Capt & adj)
	8.		Lecture to Battalion by Major M. A. JACKSON RGA. Lecture to Senior officers by Captain M. LE JEUNE RFC. Major CLWM PRICE proceeded on leave to England.	Travers (Capt & adj)
	9.		Battalion route march. LIEUT GEN: F. I. MAXSE bids formal farewell to all officers of 55th Inf: Bde who have fought with 18th Divn. Also presents ribbons for decorations. Captain H. R. LONGBOURNE DSO rejoined battalion from Senior Officers School, ALDERSHOT. Captain F. TRAVERS rejoined battalion from leave. 2/Lt FULLAGAR rejoined battalion from leave.	Travers (Capt & adj)
	10.		Company training and preparations for move to forward area.	Travers (Capt & adj)
COULONVILLERS	11.		Battalion moved by route march to COULONVILLERS and went into billets there	Travers (Capt & adj)
BOIS BERGUES	12.		Battalion moved by march route to BOIS BERGUES and went into billets there.	Travers (Capt & adj)
	13.		Nothing to record.	Travers (Capt & adj)
RAINCHEVAL	14		Battalion moved by march route to RAINCHEVAL and went into billets there	Travers (Capt & adj)
	15.		Nothing to record.	

2449 Wt. W14957/M90 750,000 1/16 J.B.C. & A. Forms/C.2118/12.

Figure 6 A typical Unit War Diary entry, this recording the arrival of 2/Lt H. J. A'Bear at 7th Battalion Queen's Royal West Surrey Regiment on 1 January 1917 (WO 95/2051)

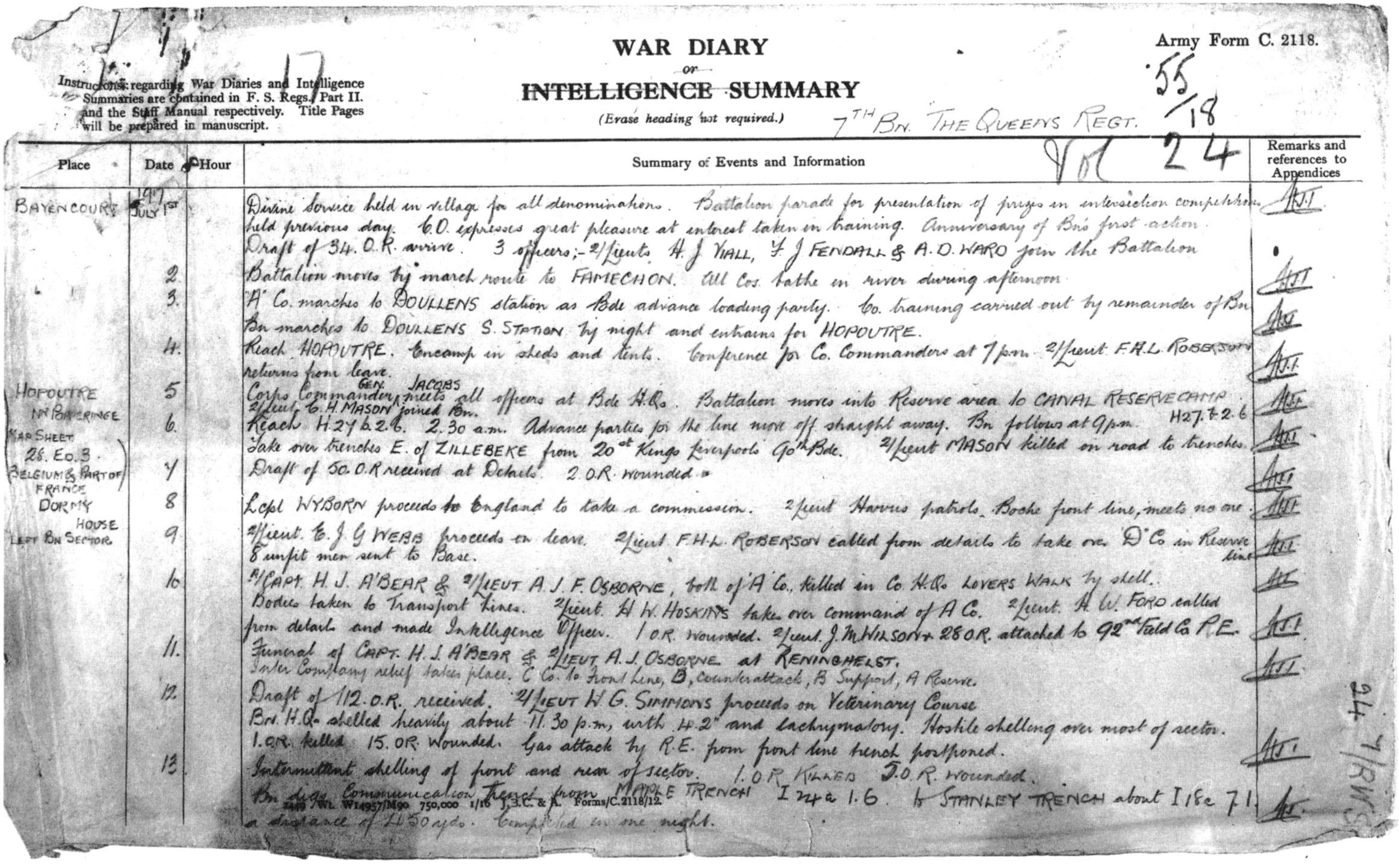

WAR DIARY

or

~~INTELLIGENCE SUMMARY~~

(Erase heading not required.)

Instructions regarding War Diaries and Intelligence Summaries are contained in F. S. Regs., Part II. and the Staff Manual respectively. Title Pages will be prepared in manuscript.

Army Form C. 2118.

7TH BN. THE QUEENS REGT.

55/18 24

Place	Date	Hour	Summary of Events and Information	Remarks and references to Appendices
BAYENCOURT	1917 JULY 1ST		Divine Service held in village for all denominations. Battalion parade for presentation of prizes in intersection competition held previous day. C.O. expresses great pleasure at interest taken in training. Anniversary of Bn's first action. Draft of 34 O.R. arrive. 3 officers; – 2/Lieuts H. J. HALL, F. J. FENDALL & A. D. WARD join the Battalion	H.J.I.
	2.		Battalion moves by march route to FAMECHON. All Cos. bathe in river during afternoon	H.J.I.
	3.		"A" Co. marches to DOULLENS station as Bde advance loading party. Co. training carried out by remainder of Bn. Bn marches to DOULLENS S. STATION by night and entrains for HOPOUTRE.	H.J.I.
	4.		Reach HOPOUTRE. Encamp in sheds and tents. Conference for Co. Commanders at 7 p.m. 2/Lieut. F.H.L. ROBERSON returns from leave.	H.J.I.
HOPOUTRE Nr POPERINGE	5		Corps Commander GEN. JACOBS meets all officers at Bde H.Q. Battalion moves into Reserve area to CANAL RESERVE CAMP. 2/Lieut. C. H. MASON joined Bn.	H.J.I.
MAP SHEET 28. Ed. 3. BELGIUM & PART OF FRANCE	6.		Reach H.27 b.2.6. 2.30 a.m. Advance parties for the line move off straight away. Bn follows at 9 p.m. H27.b.2.6	H.J.I.
	7		Take over trenches E. of ZILLEBEKE from 20th Kings Liverpools 90th Bde. 2/Lieut MASON killed on road to trenches. Draft of 50 O.R. received at Details. 2 O.R. wounded.	H.J.I.
DORMY HOUSE	8		L/cpl WYBORN proceeds to England to take a commission. 2/Lieut Harris patrols Boche front line, meets no one.	H.J.I.
LEFT BN SECTOR	9		2/Lieut. E. J. G. WEBB proceeds on leave. 2/Lieut F.H.L. ROBERSON called from details to take over "D" Co in Reserve line. 8 unfit men sent to Base.	H.J.I.
	10		A/Capt. H. J. A'BEAR & 2/LIEUT A. J. F. OSBORNE, both of 'A' Co. killed in Co. H.Q. LOVERS WALK by shell. Bodies taken to Transport Lines. 2/Lieut. H. W. HOSKINS takes over command of A Co. 2/Lieut. A. W. FORD called from detail and made Intelligence Officer. 1 O.R. wounded. 2/Lieut. J. M. WILSON + 28 O.R. attached to 92nd Field Co R.E.	H.J.I.
	11.		Funeral of CAPT. H. J. A'BEAR & 2/LIEUT A. J. OSBORNE at RENINGHELST. Inter Company relief takes place. C Co. to front line, B, counterattack, B Support, A Reserve.	H.J.I.
	12.		Draft of 112 O.R. received. 2/LIEUT H. G. SIMMONS proceeds on Veterinary Course. Bn. H.Q. shelled heavily about 11.30 p.m. with 4.2" and lachrymatory. Hostile shelling over most of sector. 1 O.R. killed 15 O.R. wounded. Gas attack by R.E. from front line trench postponed.	H.J.I.
	13		Intermittent shelling of front and rear of sector. 1 O.R. KILLED 3 O.R. wounded. Bn digs Communication Trench from MAPLE TRENCH I 24 a 1.6. to STANLEY TRENCH about I 18 c 7 1. a distance of 450 yds. Completed in one night.	H.J.I.

Wt. W14957/M90 750,000 1/16 J.B.C. & A. Forms/C.2118/12.

24 7/RWS

Figure 7 The Unit War Diary entry recording the death of H. J. A'Bear on 10 July 1917 (WO 95/2051)

After 1915 nearly all officers granted commissions had to have seen service in the ranks.

According to A'Bear's record of service he was discharged to commission on 24 December 1916. Rather than return to England for further training A'Bear was trained in France, for it is noted in the Unit War Diary of 7th Battalion Queen's Royal West Surrey Regiment (WO 95/2051) on 1 January 1917 that 2nd Lt H. J. A'Bear joined the battalion from GHQ Cadet School. See **Fig 6**.

Second Lt H. J. A'Bear first appears in the *Army List* in March 1917 on page 916 f. See **Fig 5**.

Official notification of 2nd Lt H. J. A'Bear joining his battalion in the field is preserved in his record of service. What is interesting about his commission in the field is that he rejoined his old unit, rather than being posted to a new one which frequently happened. See **Fig 3**.

Second Lt A'Bear is next noted in the Unit War Diary as leading a patrol on 23 February. Further reference to A'Bear is made on 3 June 1917 when he is noted as moving from A Company to D Company and also taking command of the company with the rank of acting Captain.

In early July, the 18th Division were holding a section of the front near Zillebeke, east-south-east of Ypres. Seventh Battalion Queen's Royal West Surrey Regiment, 55th Infantry Brigade, were holding the left flank of the Divisional position. According to the 18th Division General Headquarters diary (WO 95/2016) the division were dispersed in positions shown on 1:20000 Map 28NW/NE at I23a58.40.

The next, and unfortunately final entry in the Unit War Diary records on 10 July 1917, Captain H. J. A'Bear and 2nd Lt A. J. F. Osborne, both of A Company, killed in company HQ, Lovers Walk by shell. Captain A'Bear was one of only three officers of the battalion killed in July 1917.

Second Lt/Acting Captain H. J. A'Bear MM is buried in Reninghelst New Military Cemetery, south west of Ypres.

The remaining contents of his record of service relate to the settling of his estate and the return of his personal effects to his next of kin, Mrs H. J. A'Bear, Rectory Cottage, Hascombe, Nr Godalming.

The sources used to create this case study include the Medal Index Cards (WO 372), the *Army List*, the Unit War Diary of 7th Battalion Queen's Royal West Surrey Regiment (WO 95/2051), the Commonwealth War Graves Commission website (see section **15.4.3**) and H. J. A'Bear's record of service in WO 339/117622.

3 Other ranks' records of service

3.1 Introduction

The files preserved in the record series WO 363, WO 364, WO 398 and PIN 26 represent some 2.8 million individuals, most of whom saw operational service overseas. All of the files are unique, for while many shared a similar war experience, their careers could be so different.

The reasons why the records discussed in this chapter are the way that they are, is mentioned in section **1.2**.

There is no such thing as a normal First World War record of service. Whilst many of the records contain Army Forms, which are common to most files, the files really do vary. Some files may be a single sheet, others may run to over 60 pages. There are a number of forms, which if they are found in the file of the person you are looking for, will alone be so informative that they will provide you with most of the data you seek. It is possible, however, that you will need to refer to a number of different forms found in a record of service, together with other records discussed in this book, in order to recreate something resembling a record of service.

This chapter cannot explain all of the different types of Army Forms that can be found in these records but all those that are significant are covered below.

Originally a soldier's record would have consisted of an attestation sheet of which there are over ten different varieties depending upon date of enlistment, period of service and terms of engagement. Over seven different attestation forms can be found in either WO 363 or WO 364. The most common include the following:

- AF B 141. Short Service 3 Years
- AF B 2512. Short Service 3 Years. Duration of the War with the Colours and Reserve
- AF E 501. Territorial Force 4 Years Service in the United Kingdom
- AF B 2505. Short Service Duration of the War
- AF B 2515. Enrolment Paper and Record of Service
- AF B 311. Short Service 3 Years
- AF B 111. Short Service 1 Years Service with the Colours 3 Years Reserve

An example of an attestation form can be seen in **Fig 8**.

On all attestation papers or enrolment forms it is usual to find the information given by recruits when they went to enlist. In most cases the age and physical description of the soldier, his place of birth, any former service and occupation can be found. In some cases data concerning the next of kin may also be present. Kept within the attestation documents would usually be a conduct sheet and medical history sheet. If the soldier was a member of the Territorial Army, then an Imperial Service Obligation (AF E 624) form consenting to overseas service may be found. One of the most significant forms that might be found in a file is the Army Form B 103: Casualty Form-Active Service. On this form was recorded all of the most useful information about a soldier: his service details, his date of enlistment, promotions, awards, leave, transfers and anything else relating to him as an individual that the Army needed to know about. In short the AF B 103 contains everything you might need to know about a soldier on one piece of paper. The AF B 103 was common to the whole Army, officer and other ranks, male and female.

At the end of a man's army career he would be discharged. This entailed the completion of another set of forms. Of these forms the most useful is the Personal Protection or Identity Certificate (PIC) (Army Form Z11), which provided information about age, physical and unit details. It also gave the man's address. An example of a discharge form can be seen in **Fig 9**.

In many files it is possible to find a variety of other forms of correspondence, many of which concerned the soldier as to his employment before or after enlistment. This type of correspondence whilst not containing much information concerning the war, can provide useful information about the man, his non-military life and his family.

Using the records in WO 363 and WO 364 is like a voyage of discovery. You know what you want to find and know where to look but what you find can be disappointing or revelatory.

3.2 The 'Burnt Records' WO 363

The records in this series are the records that survived the fire at Arnside Street on 8 September 1940. Not only are they fire damaged, but also they are water damaged. Consequently the originals are so fragile, the only way they can be made available is on microfilm. How these records were arranged before the fire is unknown. However, they were put into an alphabetical sequence after the war.

The records in this series are for men who completed their service at any time between 1914 and 1920. Amongst the records can be found those of men who survived the war,

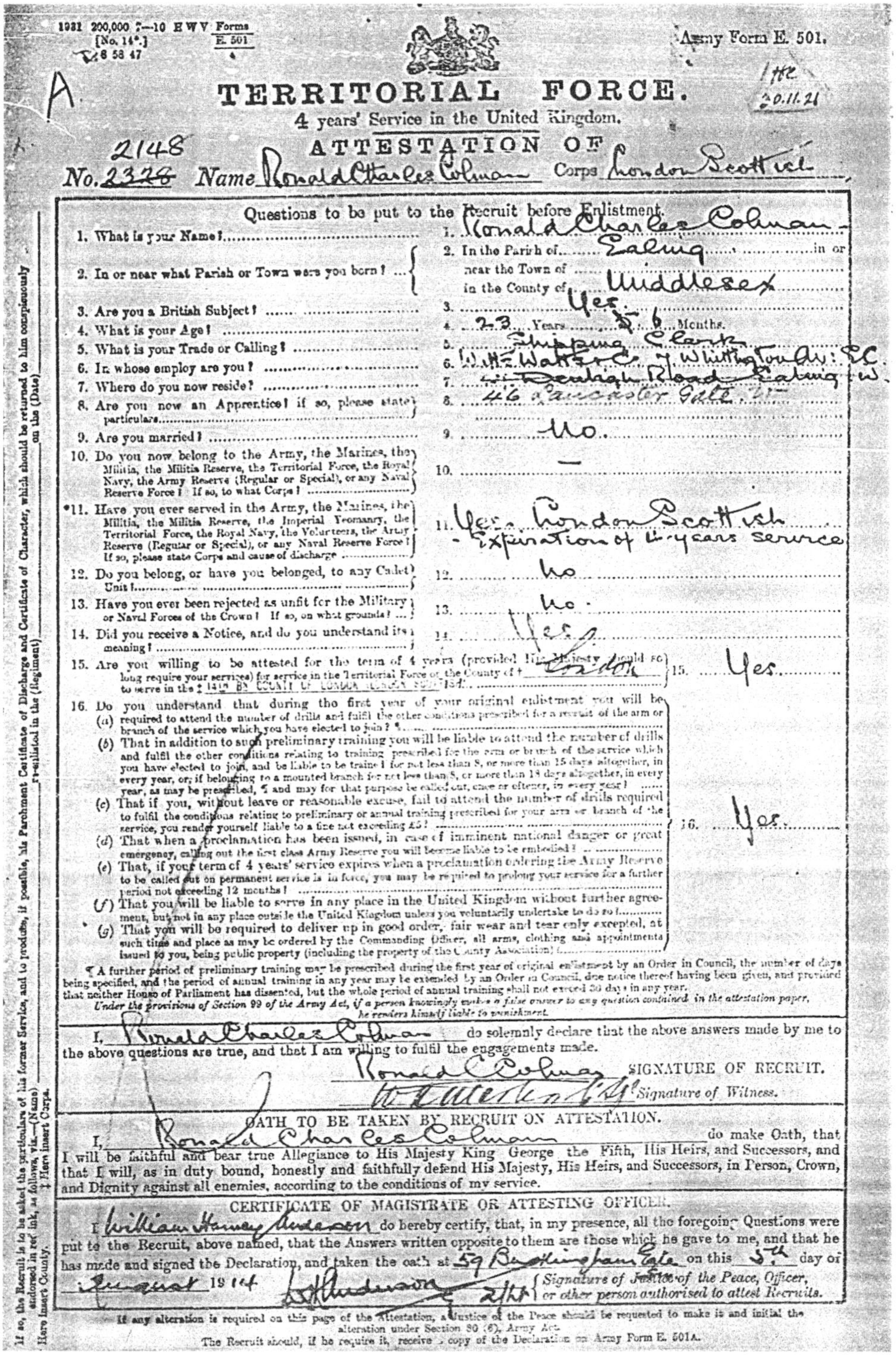

1931 200,000 7—10 H W V Forms [No. 14*.] E. 501 / 6 58 47

Army Form E. 501.

A.

1 HC 30.11.21

TERRITORIAL FORCE.

4 years' Service in the United Kingdom.

ATTESTATION OF

No. ~~2328~~ 2148 Name Ronald Charles Colman Corps London Scottish

Questions to be put to the Recruit before Enlistment.

1. What is your Name? — 1. Ronald Charles Colman
2. In or near what Parish or Town were you born? — 2. In the Parish of Ealing in or near the Town of ... in the County of Middlesex
3. Are you a British Subject? — 3. Yes
4. What is your Age? — 4. 23 Years 6 Months.
5. What is your Trade or Calling? — 5. Shipping Clerk
6. In whose employ are you? — 6. W.H. Watts & Co. 7 Whittington Av: E.C.
7. Where do you now reside? — 7. ~~Denbigh Road Ealing W.~~
8. Are you now an Apprentice? if so, please state particulars — 8. 46 Lancaster Gate W.
9. Are you married? — 9. No.
10. Do you now belong to the Army, the Marines, the Militia, the Militia Reserve, the Territorial Force, the Royal Navy, the Army Reserve (Regular or Special), or any Naval Reserve Force? If so, to what Corps? — 10. —
*11. Have you ever served in the Army, the Marines, the Militia, the Militia Reserve, the Imperial Yeomanry, the Territorial Force, the Royal Navy, the Volunteers, the Army Reserve (Regular or Special), or any Naval Reserve Force? If so, please state Corps and cause of discharge — 11. Yes. London Scottish – Expiration of 4 years service
12. Do you belong, or have you belonged, to any Cadet Unit? — 12. No
13. Have you ever been rejected as unfit for the Military or Naval Forces of the Crown? If so, on what grounds? — 13. No.
14. Did you receive a Notice, and do you understand its meaning? — 14. Yes.
15. Are you willing to be attested for the term of 4 years (provided His Majesty should so long require your services) for service in the Territorial Force of the County of † London to serve in the ‡ 14th Bn County of London Regiment ... — 15. Yes.
16. Do you understand that during the first year of your original enlistment you will be (a) required to attend the number of drills and fulfil the other conditions prescribed for a recruit of the arm or branch of the service which you have elected to join? ¶ (b) That in addition to such preliminary training you will be liable to attend the number of drills and fulfil the other conditions relating to training prescribed for the arm or branch of the service which you have elected to join, and be liable to be trained for not less than 8, or more than 15 days altogether, in every year, or, if belonging to a mounted branch for not less than 8, or more than 18 days altogether, in every year, as may be prescribed, ¶ and may for that purpose be called out, once or oftener, in every year? (c) That if you, without leave or reasonable excuse, fail to attend the number of drills required to fulfil the conditions relating to preliminary or annual training prescribed for your arm or branch of the service, you render yourself liable to a fine not exceeding £5? (d) That when a proclamation has been issued, in case of imminent national danger or great emergency, calling out the first class Army Reserve you will become liable to be embodied? (e) That, if your term of 4 years' service expires when a proclamation ordering the Army Reserve to be called out on permanent service is in force, you may be required to prolong your service for a further period not exceeding 12 months? (f) That you will be liable to serve in any place in the United Kingdom without further agreement, but not in any place outside the United Kingdom unless you voluntarily undertake to do so? (g) That you will be required to deliver up in good order, fair wear and tear only excepted, at such time and place as may be ordered by the Commanding Officer, all arms, clothing and appointments issued to you, being public property (including the property of the County Association)? — 16. Yes.

¶ A further period of preliminary training may be prescribed during the first year of original enlistment by an Order in Council, the number of days being specified, and the period of annual training in any year may be extended by an Order in Council, due notice thereof having been given, and provided that neither House of Parliament has dissented, but the whole period of annual training shall not exceed 30 days in any year.

Under the provisions of Section 99 of the Army Act, if a person knowingly makes a false answer to any question contained in the attestation paper, he renders himself liable to punishment.

I, Ronald Charles Colman do solemnly declare that the above answers made by me to the above questions are true, and that I am willing to fulfil the engagements made.

Ronald C Colman SIGNATURE OF RECRUIT.

W.H. Watts & Co *Signature of Witness.*

OATH TO BE TAKEN BY RECRUIT ON ATTESTATION.

I, Ronald Charles Colman do make Oath, that I will be faithful and bear true Allegiance to His Majesty King George the Fifth, His Heirs, and Successors, and that I will, as in duty bound, honestly and faithfully defend His Majesty, His Heirs, and Successors, in Person, Crown, and Dignity against all enemies, according to the conditions of my service.

CERTIFICATE OF MAGISTRATE OR ATTESTING OFFICER.

I William Harvey Anderson do hereby certify, that, in my presence, all the foregoing Questions were put to the Recruit, above named, that the Answers written opposite to them are those which he gave to me, and that he has made and signed the Declaration, and taken the oath at 59 Buckingham Gate on this 5th day of August 1914.

W H Anderson 2/Lt *Signature of Justice of the Peace, Officer, or other person authorised to attest Recruits.*

If any alteration is required on this page of the Attestation, a Justice of the Peace should be requested to make it and initial the alteration under Section 80 (6), Army Act.

The Recruit should, if he require it, receive a copy of the Declaration on Army Form E. 501A.

If so, the Recruit is to be asked the particulars of his former Service, and to produce, if possible, his Parchment Certificate of Discharge and Certificate of Character, which should be returned to him conspicuously endorsed in red ink, as follows, viz.—(Name) re-enlisted in the (Regiment) on the (Date)

† Here insert County. ‡ Here insert Corps.

Figure 8 A Territorial Army Attestation Form AF E 501 (WO 364/742)

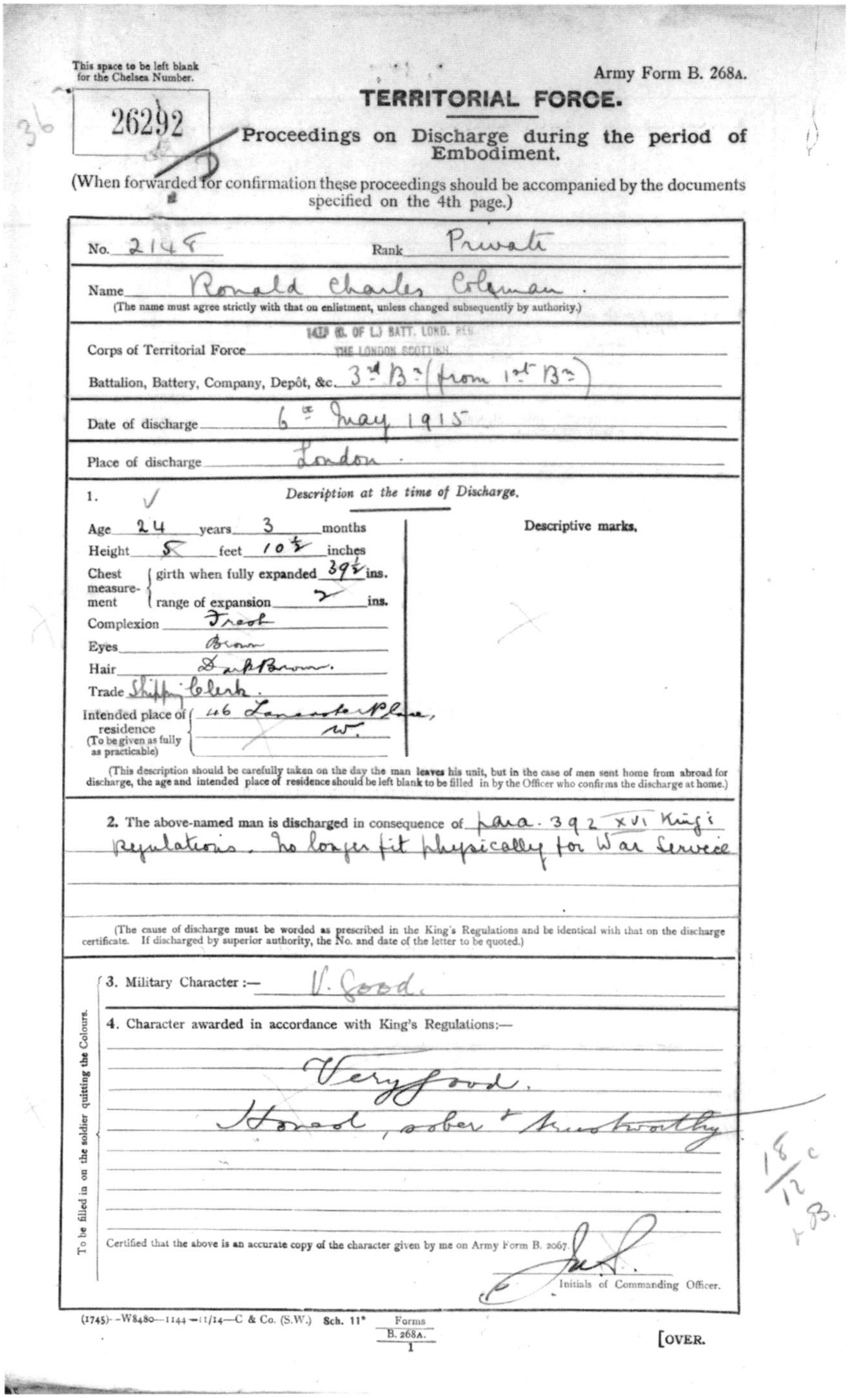

This space to be left blank for the Chelsea Number.

26292

Army Form B. 268A.

TERRITORIAL FORCE.

Proceedings on Discharge during the period of Embodiment.

(When forwarded for confirmation these proceedings should be accompanied by the documents specified on the 4th page.)

No. 2148 Rank Private

Name Ronald Charles Coleman.

(The name must agree strictly with that on enlistment, unless changed subsequently by authority.)

Corps of Territorial Force 14th (C. of L.) BATT. LOND. REG. THE LONDON SCOTTISH.

Battalion, Battery, Company, Depôt, &c. 3rd Bn (from 1st Bn)

Date of discharge 6th May 1915

Place of discharge London.

1. Description at the time of Discharge.

Age 24 years 3 months

Height 5 feet 10½ inches

Chest measurement: girth when fully expanded 39½ ins.; range of expansion 2 ins.

Complexion Fresh

Eyes Brown

Hair Dark Brown.

Trade Shipping Clerk.

Intended place of residence (To be given as fully as practicable) 46 Lancaster Place, W.

Descriptive marks.

(This description should be carefully taken on the day the man leaves his unit, but in the case of men sent home from abroad for discharge, the age and intended place of residence should be left blank to be filled in by the Officer who confirms the discharge at home.)

2. The above-named man is discharged in consequence of para. 392 XVI King's Regulations. No longer fit physically for War Service

(The cause of discharge must be worded as prescribed in the King's Regulations and be identical with that on the discharge certificate. If discharged by superior authority, the No. and date of the letter to be quoted.)

3. Military Character:— V. Good.

4. Character awarded in accordance with King's Regulations:—

Very Good.

Honest, sober & trustworthy

To be filled in on the soldier quitting the Colours.

Certified that the above is an accurate copy of the character given by me on Army Form B. 2067.

Initials of Commanding Officer.

(1745)--W8480—1144—11/14—C & Co. (S.W.) Sch. 11* Forms B. 268A. 1

[OVER.

Figure 9 A typical discharge form AF B 268a (WO 364/742)

men who died of wounds or disease and men who were killed in action. Also in WO 363 there are a number of files of men who were executed, including Joseph Stones and William Nelson. Many of the files concern men who were discharged as a result of sickness or wounds contracted or received during the war.

3.2.1 Arrangement

The original records in WO 363 are kept in 33,000 boxes. As the collection is so big, the only way it could be filmed was by letter of the alphabet. As there are a number of cameras doing the filming, the filming of the range of surnames of any given letter is not just started at the first name and then done in sequence – each camera has been given a specific range of surnames within a letter. As this is the case it is very important to consult the WO 363 catalogue for the letter of the alphabet you want and then find the relevant surname and forename(s). The first reel of WO 363 S (WO 363/S1), for example, may not cover a surname beginning with Sa but may start at Sl. All of the catalogues in WO 363 are arranged in alphabetical order by surname and not in piece number order.

> **WO 363 example**
> *This list shows the names in alphabetical order and the type of jump between piece numbers which occurs.*
>
> | WO 363/C17 | Cainey, Arthur–Cairney, Andrew |
> | WO 363/C29 | Cairney, Charles–Cairns, Alexander |

Although the microfilming of WO 363 will not be completed until the summer of 2002, the following statistics indicate the enormous size of this particular record collection and its associated problems:

Number of reels of microfilm per letter

Letter	Reels	Letter	Reels	Letter	Reels
A	738	B	2679	C	1955
D	1143	E	609	F	1025
N	398	O	299	P	1717
Q	36	R	1750	S	3327
T	1405	U	45	V	117
W	2451	Y	138	Z	5

Included in the figure for surnames beginning with the letter S are 562 reels of Smith including 52 reels of John Smith!

3.3 The 'Unburnt Records' WO 364

The records in WO 364 are those records that the War Office recovered from other government departments at the end of the Second World War. The majority of these records came from the Ministry of Pensions and they primarily concern men who were discharged from the army on account of sickness or wounds suffered between 1914 and 1920. A large number of files concern soldiers who had been discharged to pension before the war and who by virtue of further service between 1914 and 1920, needed to have their pension payments altered on account of additional service.

WO 364 also contains a number of very interesting anomalies. Records of a number of soldiers who were discharged many years before the First World War, as far back as 1875, have been found in WO 364. A number of files of British men who served in the South African Infantry or Australian Imperial Force but who were discharged in Britain have also been found in this record series.

Most of the files in WO 364 contain not only the usual military type records relating to enlistment, conduct and overseas service, but also detailed medical records relating to the disability for which the individual was granted a pension. Many of these medical records contain descriptions of wounds and the date and place the soldiers were when they were wounded. This information can be used when looking at the unit war diaries in WO 95.

3.3.1 Arrangement

Unlike WO 363 which is arranged by letter and then by name, WO 364 is arranged in alphabetical order. There are four A–Z sequences in WO 364:

- WO 364/1–4912   A–Z
- WO 364/4913–4915   A–Z
- WO 364/5000–5802   A–Z
- WO 364/5803–5804   A–W miss sorts

3.4 Women's Auxiliary Army Corps WO 398

Conceived in early 1917, and formally established by Army Council Instruction No 1068 of July 1917, the Women's Auxiliary Army Corps (WAAC) was established upon the recommendations of Lieutenant General H. M. Lawson, who suggested that women be employed in France.

W16847- 9293/1 20,000 3/17 HWV(P2062)

Army Form W. 3578.

FORM OF ENROLMENT IN THE WOMEN'S ARMY AUXILIARY CORPS.

No. _681_ Name (Mrs. or Miss) ~~Miss~~ (Christian) _Agnes May_

Surname _Worsdall_

Questions to be put to the Woman on enrolment.

1. What is your name? ... ...   1. _Agnes May Worsdall_

2. What is your age? ... ...   2. _24_

3. What is your permanent postal address? ...   3. _9. Western Rd Derby._

You are hereby warned that if after enrolment it is found that you have wilfully given a false answer to any of the following questions, the Army Council or any person duly authorized by them retain the right to terminate any contract that they may have entered into with you.

4. Are both your parents British-born subjects?   4. _yes_

5. Do you agree to be enrolled in the Women's Army Auxiliary Corps, and fulfil the regulations and instructions laid down from time to time for this Corps? ... ...   5. _yes._

6. Are you single, married, or a widow? ...   6. _Single._

7. Have you any dependants? ... ...   7. _no_

8. Are you willing to be vaccinated and inoculated? ... ...   8. _yes._

9. Are you willing to be enrolled for service abroad? ... ...   9. _yes._

10. Do you undertake to work wherever the Army Council may require? ... ...   10. _yes._

Figure 10 Army Form W 3578 WAAC Enrolment Form (WO 398/237)

Organized into four sections: Cookery, Mechanical, Clerical and Miscellaneous, the women in the corps were split into 'Officials' (the officers) and 'Members' (the other ranks). Renamed the Queen Mary's Army Auxiliary Corps in April 1918, the corps would eventually employ some 57,000 women at home and overseas. Those women who served at Royal Flying Corps airfields transferred to the Women's Royal Air Force when it was created in April 1918. Approximately 10,000 women transferred and their records can be found in AIR 80.

Most files in WO 398 contain an Army Form W 3578 Form of Enrolment in the Women's Army Auxiliary Corps. This form provides information such as the age of the woman, her address, marital status and whether she was willing to serve overseas. If the member of the WAAC served overseas then an Army Form B 103 may be found.

One of the most informative forms which occur in WO 398 is the NSVW 3 National Service Department (Women's Section) Qualifications of Applicant form. This form tells you where the woman was born, her current address, any qualifications and work experience and current occupation and the names of two referees.

As with all other service personnel, women also had an identification certificate, an Army Form W 3577, which gave a physical description and the home address of the holder.

The records in WO 398 comprise the surviving records of service of female other ranks of the Women's Auxiliary Army Corps (Queen Mary's Auxiliary Army Corps). There are no surviving records of service of female officers of the corps.

3.5 The Ministry of Pensions records PIN 26

In PIN 26 are preserved 22,801 files of officers and other ranks, male and female, Army and Royal Navy, who were discharged from the services as a result of sickness or wounds contracted or received during the war. This record series also includes a number of files of dependants rather than the service personnel themselves. PIN 26 is only a 2 per cent sample of all of the files concerning service personnel who had pensions that were granted or administered by the Ministry of Pensions. However, a significant percentage of the remaining 98 per cent from which this sample was taken, can actually be found in WO 364.

The records in PIN 26 are arranged in a number of series within the collection. In most cases they are arranged in alphabetical order and in many cases the catalogue provides basic data about the reason for discharge.

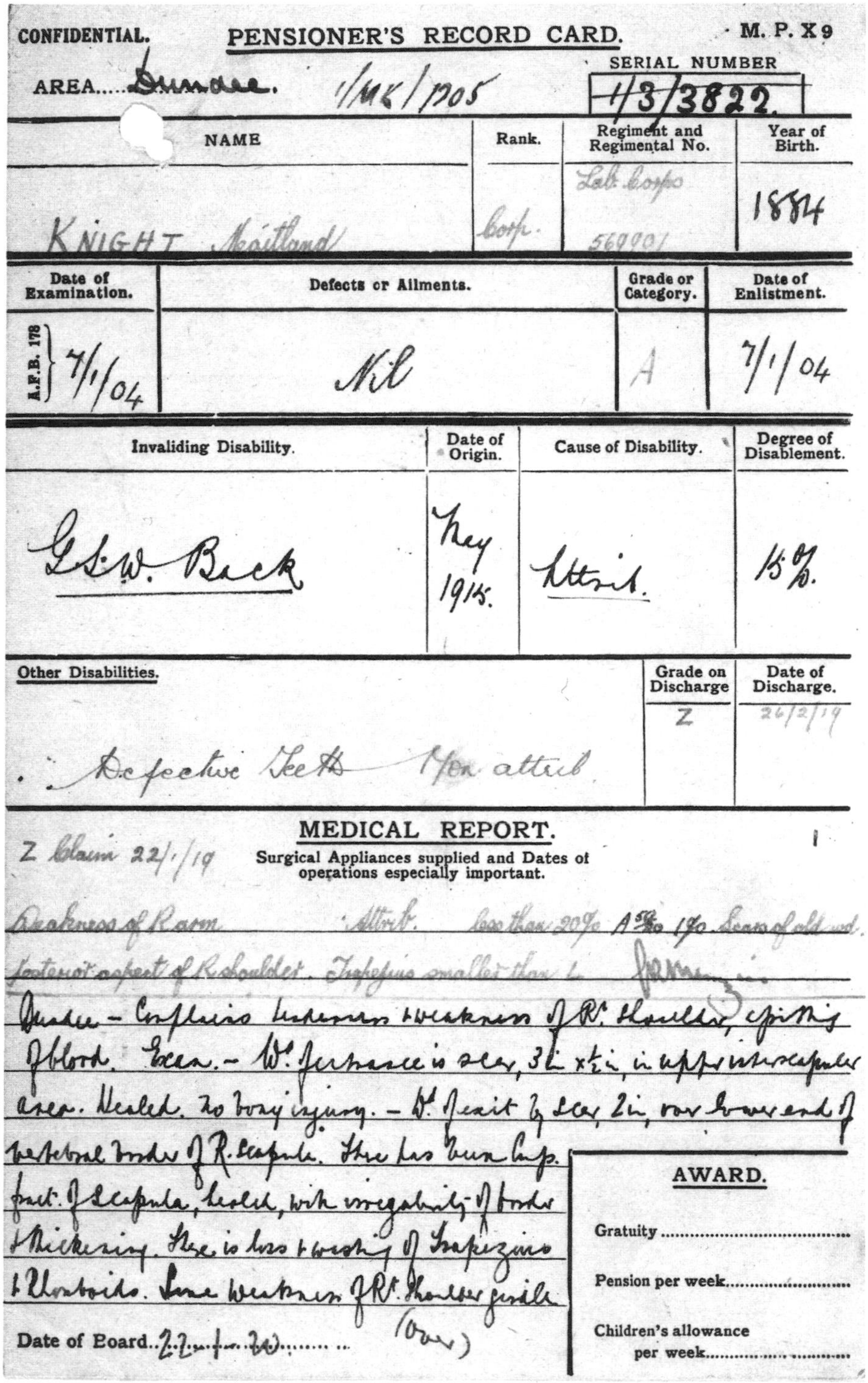

CONFIDENTIAL. PENSIONER'S RECORD CARD. M. P. X9

AREA Dundee. 1/MK/1705

SERIAL NUMBER 1/3/3822.

NAME	Rank.	Regiment and Regimental No.	Year of Birth.
KNIGHT Maitland	Corp.	Lab. Corps 569901	1884

Date of Examination.	Defects or Ailments.	Grade or Category.	Date of Enlistment.
A.F.B. 178 7/1/04	Nil	A	7/1/04

Invaliding Disability.	Date of Origin.	Cause of Disability.	Degree of Disablement.
G.S.W. Back	May 1915.	Attrib.	15%.

Other Disabilities.	Grade on Discharge	Date of Discharge.
Defective Teeth Non attrib	Z	26/2/19

MEDICAL REPORT.

Z Claim 22/1/19

Surgical Appliances supplied and Dates of operations especially important.

Weakness of R arm Attrib. less than 20% ... Scar of old wd. posterior aspect of R shoulder. Trapezius smaller than L ...

Dundee – Complains ... weakness of Rt. shoulder, spitting of blood. Exam. – Wd. entrance is scar, 3 in x ½ in, in upper interscapular area. Healed. No bony injury. – Wd. exit by scar, 2 in, over lower end of vertebral border of R. scapula. There has been comp. fract. of scapula, healed, with irregularity of border & thickening. There is loss & wasting of trapezius & rhomboids. Some weakness of Rt. shoulder girdle (Over)

Date of Board 22 – 1 – 20

AWARD.

Gratuity ....

Pension per week..........

Children's allowance per week..........

Figure 11 ORs' (Other Ranks') Disability (PIN 26/8568)

One point to note about PIN 26 is the date range given for each file. As the files concern disability pensions paid to individuals, the dates given reflect the date an individual joined the armed forces and the date the pension ceased.

Amongst the files in PIN 26 are the records concerning a soldier who won the Victoria Cross at the defence of Rorke's Drift in January 1879, during the Zulu War, and a file for a soldier who was eventually hanged as a murderer. Both individuals saw service between 1914 and 1918.

The actual paper content of the files in PIN 26 is very similar to the records in WO 364; basic record of service, medical reports and assessments and pension calculations and awards. As in many cases the pensions ceased upon death of the individual, the files often contain death certificates.

The content of PIN 26 is arranged in the following sections, all of which are arranged in alphabetical order:

- PIN 26/1–16683   Other ranks
- PIN 26/19854–19923   Other ranks
- PIN 26/20287–21065   Pensioners living overseas
- PIN 26/22757–22800   Other ranks
- PIN 26/19955–19984   Alternative disabled pensions

3.6 Files of dead Chelsea pensioners WO 324

WO 324 is a collection of some 269 files of soldiers who were at one time inmates at the Royal Hospital Chelsea. Arranged in alphabetical order, the files are more concerned with the soldiers' time in the hospital than with their military careers, although brief information about their service is usually included. The dates of the files reflect the dates when they entered the hospital and the dates when they died, not their service dates.

3.7 The King's African Rifles and West African Frontier Force

During the First World War a large number of British Army NCOs served as instructors in either the King's African Rifles (KAR) or the West African Frontier Force (WAFF) (either the Gold Coast Regiment, the Nigeria Regiment or Sierra Leone Battalion). A number of these men were serving at the outbreak of the war; many volunteered after the war had started.

The correspondence of the West African Frontier Force, which includes plenty of information about operations of the WAFF and the soldiers serving in it, can be found in CO 445. The correspondence of the King's African Rifles can be found in CO 534.

A list of British Army NCOs serving in the KAR in September 1918, giving name, rank, number, parent regiment, battalion of the KAR and when they joined the KAR, can be found in CO 534/26 ff373–422.

3.8 The British West Indies Regiment

Although men of the British West Indies Regiment (BWIR) can be found in the medal records (see **Chapter 9**), none of their records of service have been found in either WO 363 or WO 364. Some information about men of the BWIR can be found in CO 318 Colonial Office West Indies: General Correspondence. Examples of these records include a number of nominal rolls for 1915–16 which can be found in CO 318/336, including a roll of the Bermuda Volunteer Rifle Corps, lists of wives eligible for separation pay and details of next of kin.

3.9 Case studies

Agnes May Wordsall was born in Leicester on 28 August 1892. Little is known about her prior to when she enlisted in the WAAC but she had been working as a clerk and typist for 10 years before her enlistment on 6 March 1917. On enlistment Wordsall was living with her mother at 9 Western Road, Derby and was described as 5 feet 3½ inches tall, of medium build, with mid brown hair and grey/blue eyes. She was 24 years old and was single.

Given the WAAC number 681, Wordsall volunteered for service overseas and in June 1917 she sailed for France from Folkestone. By going to France Wordsall qualified for a British War and Victory Medal.

Little is known of her service in France, however from her AF B 103 she is recorded as being in hospital at Etaples in February 1918. Granted leave to the UK in August 1918, Wordsall returned to France and served there until at least October 1919. Agnes May Wordsall served in the army until 20 November 1919 when her engagement expired.

Whilst little is known of her ability in the army, she must have been very good at her job, for on 3 June 1919 she was awarded the Medal of the Order of the British Empire, which went on to be announced in the *London Gazette* on 28 January 1920.

Agnes May Wordsall's papers can be found in WO 398/237.

The following individual is not related to the author, but just provides a typical example of a soldier's career that can be found in WO 363 or WO 364.

William Henry Spencer was born at Nechells in Birmingham in 1892. He joined the Army in the rush of volunteers on 28 September 1914. Although on his attestation form his occupation was given as Electroplater and Silver Finisher, W. H. Spencer opted to join the Royal Army Medical Corps and was given the service number 38280. At the time of his attestation Spencer was described as 5 feet 6 inches tall with a fresh complexion, blue eyes and black hair.

Unlike many of the men who joined the army in the first months of the war, Private Spencer was not single, having married Louise Greenway at Nechells on 16 December 1911. He was also a father, his son Howard William Spencer having been born at Aston in Birmingham on 25 October 1913.

According to the Army Form B 103 Casualty Form – Active Service, Private Spencer joined 55 Field Ambulance and sailed for France on 26 July 1915. This unit was part of 18 Division. Private Spencer saw service with this unit until 1918 when he transferred to 42 Field Ambulance.

Other information contained in Private Spencer's records includes the fact that he was punished on two occasions, once for being drunk and once for insubordination and not complying with an order. For these offences he was given 14 days confined to barracks and the loss of the one good conduct badge that he had been awarded on 28 September 1916.

The AF B 103 notes a number of periods of leave and also records that he was admitted as a patient to 55 Field Ambulance suffering from gonorrhoea on 16 September 1918.

Private Spencer served in the army for 4 years 179 days, including the period 25 July 1915 – 13 March 1919 overseas. Awarded the 1914/15 Star, British War Medal and Victory Medal, he was finally discharged on 12 April 1919.

Private Spencer's record of service can be found in WO 363/S 1520.

4 Nurses

4.1 Introduction

Although numerous nurses from a variety of different organizations saw service during the First World War, only the records of those nurses who were military nurses are discussed here. The records of nurses of the Voluntary Aid Detachments (VADs) are held by the Red Cross archives (see section **15.4.6**).

At the outbreak of the First World War there were two army nursing services: the Queen Alexandra's Imperial Military Nursing Service (QAIMNS) and the Territorial Force Nursing Service (TFNS). The QAIMNS was also split into two parts, the regulars and the reserve, the QAIMNS(R). The QAIMNS was established by Royal Warrant on 27 March 1902 from the Army Nursing Service (ANS) and the TFNS was formed in 1908 to support the Territorial Army, which had been created under the Territorial Reserve Forces Act of 1907.

Although nurses served in most operational theatres, only a list of those arriving in France is known (WO 95/3982). To discover if a nurse served overseas it is necessary to locate either a record of service or a campaign medal index card.

4.2 Records of service

The records of service of military nurses can be found in the record series WO 399. They are arranged in two sections: QAIMNS with the QAIMNS(R), and the TFNS. Both sections are then arranged alphabetically.

Although the series list for WO 399 describes the dates of the records as covering 1914–22, they actually cover the careers of those nurses whose service was completed prior to 1939. As long as the nurse saw no service either during or later than the Second World War, then the record may be in WO 399.

WO 339 contains the records of 15,792 nurses. The records of the QAIMNS and QAIMNS(R) are in WO 399/1–9349 and the records of the TFNS are in WO 399/9350–15792. Although the records are arranged in alphabetical order, for those nurses who married during their service, it is possible to find files listed under the later married name rather than the maiden name under which many of them started their service.

4.3 Medals

Any nurse who served in an operational theatre was eligible for the same campaign medal as her male counterparts. See **Chapter 9** for details about campaign medals. Although nurses had officer status they were not eligible for officers' gallantry awards. Nurses were eligible for the Military Medal (MM) and the Royal Red Cross (RRC). Nurses were also eligible for awards under the Most Excellent Order of the British Empire. For information about the MM and RRC and other awards for gallantry and meritorious service, see **Chapter 10**.

4.4 Disability pensions PIN 26

A small number of disability pensions files kept by the Ministry of Pensions about nurses who were given pensions on account of wounds or sickness, received or contracted during the war, can be found in PIN 26/19985–20286. These files are in alphabetical order.

4.5 Case study

Frances Maud Rice was born in 1874, the daughter of Colonel Cecil Rice, formerly of the 72nd Foot (Seaforth Highlanders), who had seen active service in the Crimea 1854–6 and the Indian Mutiny 1857–8. At the time when she became a military nurse her father was living at Kingscott House, East Grinstead in Sussex.

Although there is no information stating when she qualified as a nurse, the earliest indication that Sister Rice was already a nurse at the outbreak of the First World War is a letter dated 26 August 1914 from a Captain in the RAMC (T) at 4th General Hospital RAMC(T), certifying that she is fit for foreign service. Two days later Sister Rice officially offers her services to the Secretary of State for War (**Fig 12**). The acceptance of this offer led to Sister Rice joining the Territorial Force Nursing Service (TFNS).

Sister Rice embarked for France on 24 September 1914 and arrived there on the 26th, where she joined 5 General Hospital. By entering France before 22 November 1914, Sister Rice qualified for the 1914 Star.

During the next two years Sister Rice was to see extensive service at a number of

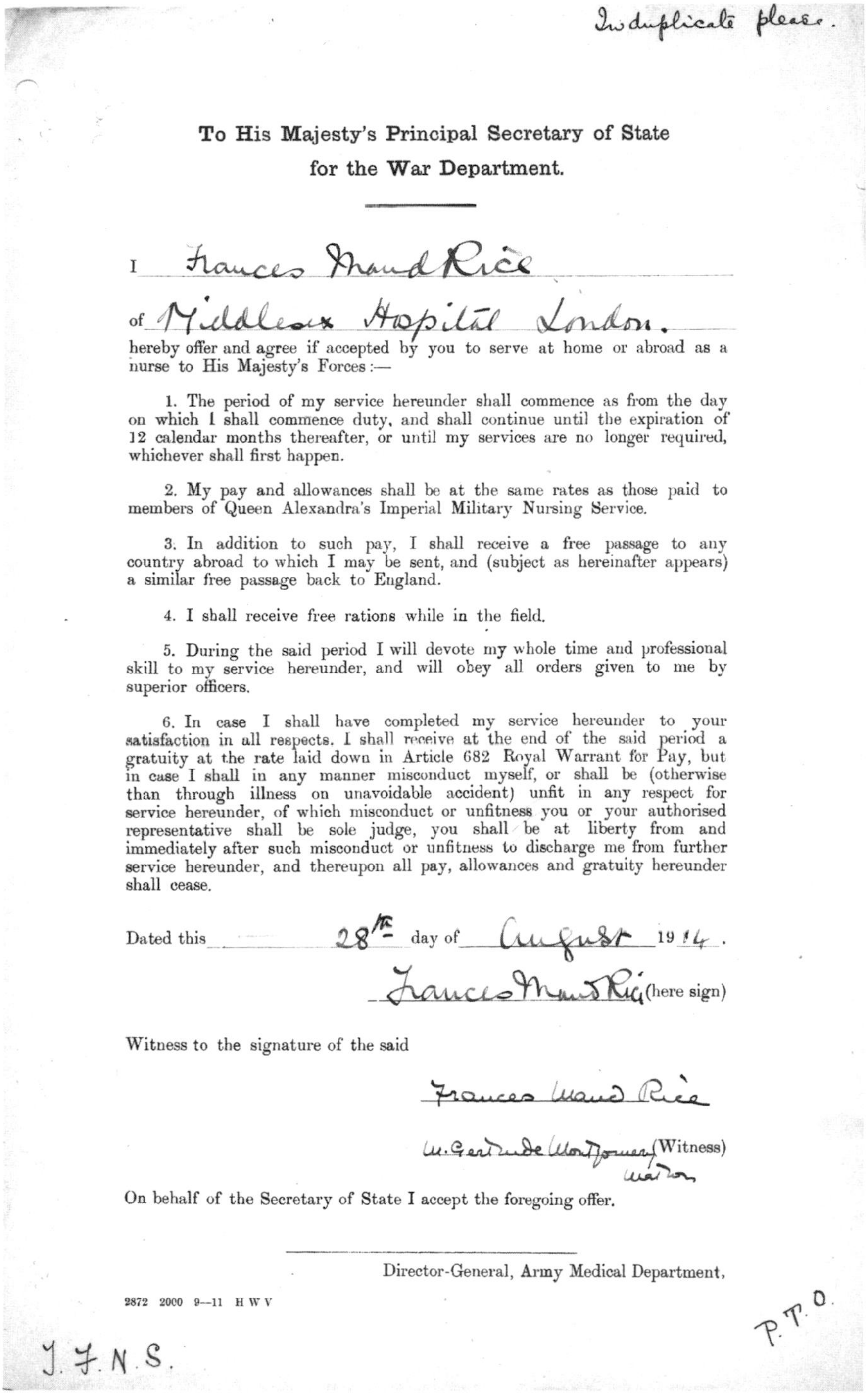

In duplicate please.

To His Majesty's Principal Secretary of State
for the War Department.

I *Frances Maud Rice*

of *Middlesex Hospital London.*

hereby offer and agree if accepted by you to serve at home or abroad as a
nurse to His Majesty's Forces :—

1. The period of my service hereunder shall commence as from the day
on which I shall commence duty, and shall continue until the expiration of
12 calendar months thereafter, or until my services are no longer required,
whichever shall first happen.

2. My pay and allowances shall be at the same rates as those paid to
members of Queen Alexandra's Imperial Military Nursing Service.

3. In addition to such pay, I shall receive a free passage to any
country abroad to which I may be sent, and (subject as hereinafter appears)
a similar free passage back to England.

4. I shall receive free rations while in the field.

5. During the said period I will devote my whole time and professional
skill to my service hereunder, and will obey all orders given to me by
superior officers.

6. In case I shall have completed my service hereunder to your
satisfaction in all respects. I shall receive at the end of the said period a
gratuity at the rate laid down in Article 682 Royal Warrant for Pay, but
in case I shall in any manner misconduct myself, or shall be (otherwise
than through illness on unavoidable accident) unfit in any respect for
service hereunder, of which misconduct or unfitness you or your authorised
representative shall be sole judge, you shall be at liberty from and
immediately after such misconduct or unfitness to discharge me from further
service hereunder, and thereupon all pay, allowances and gratuity hereunder
shall cease.

Dated this _____ 28th day of *August* 19 14.

Frances Maud Rice (here sign)

Witness to the signature of the said

Frances Maud Rice

M. Gertrude Montgomery (Witness)
Matron

On behalf of the Secretary of State I accept the foregoing offer.

_____

Director-General, Army Medical Department,

2872 2000 9—11 H W V

P.T.O.

T.F.N.S.

Figure 12 Form used by F. M. Rice to offer her services as a nurse
(WO 399/6979)

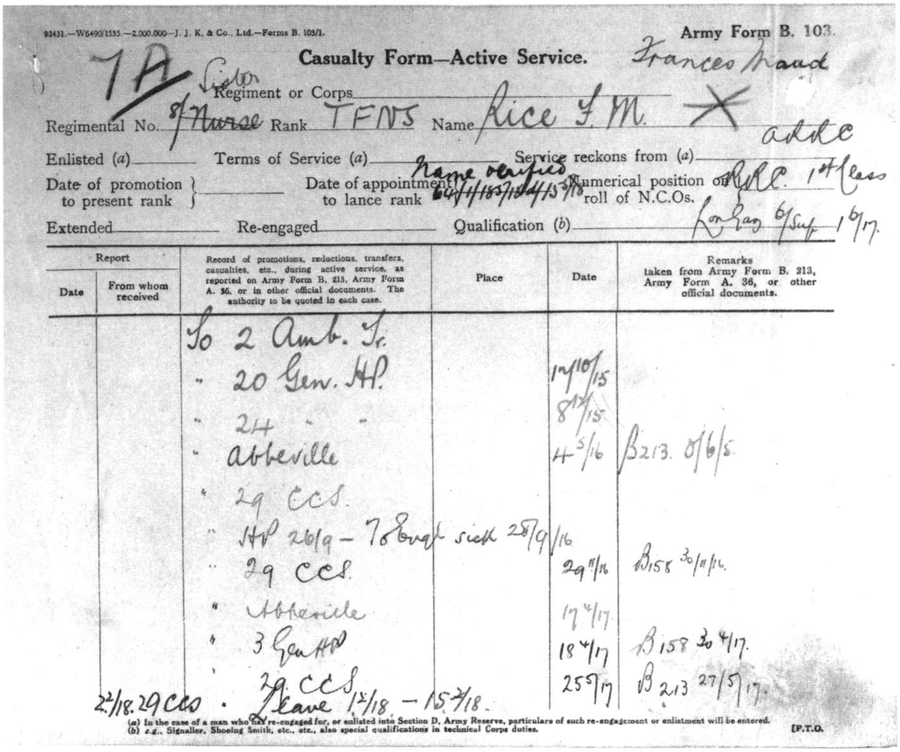

92431.—W6490/1535.—2,000,000—J. J. K. & Co., Ltd.—Forms B. 103/1.

Army Form B. 103.

Casualty Form—Active Service. Frances Maud

7A Sister

Regiment or Corps

Regimental No. S/Nurse Rank TFNS Name Rice F. M. X addc

Enlisted (a) Terms of Service (a) Name verified Service reckons from (a)

Date of promotion to present rank Date of appointment to lance rank Numerical position on roll of N.C.Os. RRC 1st Class

Extended Re-engaged Qualification (b) Lon Gaz 6/Sep 1917.

Report: Date	Report: From whom received	Record of promotions, reductions, transfers, casualties, etc., during active service, as reported on Army Form B. 213, Army Form A. 36, or in other official documents. The authority to be quoted in each case.	Place	Date	Remarks taken from Army Form B. 213, Army Form A. 36, or other official documents.
		To 2 Amb. Tr.			
		" 20 Gen. HP.		1/10/15	
		" 24 " "		8/12/15	
		" Abbeville		4/5/16	B213. 0/6/5.
		" 29 CCS.			
		" HP 26/9 – To Engl sick 28/9/16			
		" 29 CCS.		29/11/16	B158 30/11/16.
		" Abbeville		17/4/17	
		" 3 Gen HP		18/4/17	B158 30/4/17.
		" 29 CCS		25/5/17	B213 27/5/17.
2/2/18. 29 CCS		· Leave 1/2/18 – 15/2/18.			

(a) In the case of a man who has re-engaged for, or enlisted into Section D, Army Reserve, particulars of such re-engagement or enlistment will be entered.
(b) e.g., Signaller, Shoeing Smith, etc., etc., also special qualifications in technical Corps duties.

[P.T.O.

Figure 13 Casualty Form – Active Service. Army Form B 103 for F. M. Rice (WO 399/6979)

different medical units on the Western Front. After service at 5 General Hospital she went to 2 Ambulance Train, 20 General Hospital, 24 General Hospital and 29 Casualty Clearing Station. On 28 September 1916, whilst at 29 Casualty Clearing Station, Sister Rice was invalided back to England with an infected thumb.

Although the injury did not completely stop Sister Rice from working, it did necessitate a period of rest. Whilst in England Sister Rice continued to work as best she could, at the Middlesex Hospital.

After a medical board held at Millbank on 21 November 1916, Sister Rice was assessed fit and returned to France on 29 November to rejoin 29 Casualty Clearing Station.

Apart from a brief period of leave and another short period of sick leave Frances Rice was to remain nursing in France until 15 March 1919.

For her devotion to duty as a nurse Sister Frances Rice was mentioned in despatches and on 3 June 1917 was awarded the Royal Red Cross (see the **Frontispiece**). The award of the RRC was bestowed upon Sister Rice by the King in early February 1918

Figure 14 Photograph from the *Nursing Times* showing Sister F. M. Rice (middle figure) leaving Buckingham Palace after receiving her Royal Red Cross (Courtesy of the British Library, Newspaper Library)

and she was photographed coming out of Buckingham Palace after the investiture. The photograph was published in the *Nursing Times* on 16 February 1918 (see **Fig 14**).

Nothing is known of Sister Frances Maud Rice after March 1919, when information in her record of service ends.

5 Indian Army records of service

5.1 Introduction

The majority of records concerning the Indian Army are held by the Oriental and India Office Collections section of the British Library. The records discussed in this chapter relate primarily to the records held by the Public Record Office but also cover the key records held by the British Library.

Although the Indian Army was in existence for many years prior to the First World War, rather than cover numerous records, many of which will not necessarily contain data about individuals you may seek, this chapter concentrates on the most significant sources only. For those who wish to research Indian Army personnel more fully, the best guide is *Guide to the Records of the India Office Military Department* by Anthony Farrington (London 1982).

5.2 Officers

Officers in the Indian Army fall into two distinct categories: European officers and Indian officers. Unless otherwise stated the records discussed in this section relate to European officers only.

During the First World War officers and former officers of the Indian Army saw service not only with their own army, but also in, rather than just alongside, the British Army.

When war broke out in August 1914, there were a large number of serving Indian Army officers in the United Kingdom on leave. There were also many retired Indian Army officers living in the United Kingdom after completing their service. When the war started, many men from these two groups answered their country's call by either helping to fill the shortfall of officers needed in regiments and corps being sent to France, or becoming officers in many of the new units formed during the war.

To be added to these officers must be those already serving with units in India and then the records of those other ranks of the British Army who obtained commissions in the Indian Army at some stage during the war.

5.2.1 *Records held by the Public Record Office*

The Public Record Office has two key record series containing the records of service of officers who saw service during the First World War. The two series, WO 339 and WO 374, are more fully described in **Chapter 2**. However, there are two points which require further elaboration regarding Indian Army officers.

The index of officers' records of service in WO 338 (see section **2.3**) provides data which needs to be used in order to find a record of service in WO 339. Under the column for regiment or corps, instead of a numerical code for a regiment or an abbreviation for a corps, the abbreviation I.A. representing Indian Army will be found.

The records of service of those British Army other ranks who obtained commissions in the Indian Army between 1914 and 1918 can be found in WO 339/139092–139906 (Long Numbers 289026–289995). In the WO 339 catalogue they are listed at the end, rather than being dispersed throughout the whole record series.

Unfortunately research into the careers of these particular officers will need to be completed by consulting records held by the PRO and the British Library, the reason being that the records held by the PRO contain their other ranks records together with the application papers for a commission and nothing more. Once an individual was commissioned into the Indian Army, records concerning his career were the responsibility of the India Office and not the War Office. Hence the need to use the records at the British Library in the record series L/MIL/9 and L/MIL/14.

5.2.2 *Records held by the British Library*

Information about accessing the records held by the British Library can be found in section **15.4**.

The series L/MIL/9 and L/MIL/14 consist of a variety of records relating to entry and service in the East India Company and the Indian Army.

Rather than describe all of the records in these series, only information concerning those records likely to contain information about those officers who may have seen service in the First World War will be covered.

Application forms for Queen's Cadetships 1858–1930 containing biographical information about the potential officer can be found in L/MIL/9/292–302.

Indian Army officers who joined as Indian Army Unattached List cadets at Sandhurst between 1898 and 1918 are recorded in L/MIL/9/303–311. A list of these cadets for the period 1914–18 is in L/MIL/9/318.

Between 1915 and 1918, a number of cadets went to the Indian Army colleges at Wellington and Quetta. Details concerning these cadets, their family backgrounds and certificates of age can be found in L/MIL/9/320–332.

A collection of papers concerning those men granted temporary commissions in the Indian Army or the Indian Army Reserve of Officers may be found in L/MIL/9/435–623. These papers provide basic information about the man, when he was commissioned, which units he served with and when he was released.

Indian Army Statements of Service are preserved in the series L/MIL/14. There is a name index of the papers in this series on the open shelves in the India Office Reading Room in the British Library.

Service Statements for the period 1892–1916 are in the series L/MIL/14/1–49 and they contain printed forms with details about the officer, his service leave and pension.

Information about the promotion of officers can be found in L/MIL/14/61–76 covering the period 1890–1918.

Many British Army NCOs served on the Indian Unattached List in a variety of capacities. Lists of these men can be found in L/MIL/14/144–158 covering the period 1908–22. These lists provide the date of original attestation into the British Army, if applicable, the original unit served in, the Indian Army units served in and any appropriate remarks.

5.3 The *Indian Army List*

The library of the Public Record Office holds an incomplete run of the *Indian Army List* from 1902 to 1939. In most cases, however, it is possible to find the officer and therefore the information you seek.

The *Indian Army Lists* held in the PRO Library are similar to the quarterly British *Army List*, in as much as they are published in the same months: January, April, July and October. See section **2.7** for further information about the *Army List*.

As with the British *Army List*, the *Indian Army List* contains a name index that provides the relevant page number(s) for each officer who can be found in the list. One useful aspect of the Indian *Army List* over its British equivalent is the amount of information it contains about officers' qualifications. Identified by numerical codes that are listed in the front of each list, most Indian Army Officers were qualified in a diverse range of skills, e.g. languages, unlike many of their British counterparts.

5.4 Other ranks

Unfortunately very little information about native Indian Army other ranks is available in the United Kingdom. If the individual was awarded a gallantry medal some information may be gained by consulting the appropriate records (see **Chapter 10**). Similarly some information may be found in the campaign medal records (see **Chapter 9**) and operational records (see **Chapter 7**).

5.5 Case study

John Hugh McCudden was born on 31 January 1881 at Gya in Bengal, India, son of Edmund Gerald McCudden and Marion Jane McCudden. He was educated at Rossall School and by W. Arrowsmith, Military Tutor, in Edinburgh, between 1894 and August 1899 when he applied for entry into the Royal Military College by examination. At the time of his application McCudden was living at 18 Grosvenor Crescent, Edinburgh and he stated on his application that he wished to join the infantry.

Commissioned as 2/Lt on 8 January 1901 and appointed to the Indian Army on 7 April 1902, J. H. McCudden joined the 127th Baluch Light Infantry. Having seen operational service in Somaliland between 1908 and 1910, by the time of the First World War he had joined the 21st Prince Albert Victor's Own Cavalry. By the time he was promoted Major in 1916 McCudden was qualified in musketry, the machine-gun and signalling, with certificates in veterinary care, equitation, and linguistic skills in Baluchi, Persian and Pushtu.

Seeing further operational service, this time in Mesopotamia, Major McCudden went on to win the Military Cross in 1916 for 'Conspicuous gallantry when assisting in an attempt to bring in an Indian officer under heavy fire. He also showed great skill and courage when covering a retirement. He had 3 horses shot under him during the day.' The award of the MC was announced in the *London Gazette* on 16 May 1916.

For further service in Mesopotamia, Major McCudden was awarded the DSO and was mentioned in Despatches three times.

Serving on after the war, Major J. H. McCudden DSO, MC was to see further operational service during the third Afghan War of 1919.

915   **INDIAN CAVALRY.**

21st Prince Albert Victor's Own Cavalry (Frontier Force) (Daly's Horse).

Raised at Peshawar in 1849, by Lt. H. Daly, as the 1st Regt. of Punjab Cavalry. Became 1st Regt. of Cavalry, Punjab Irregular Force, 1851 ; the 1st Regt. of Cavalry, Punjab Frontier Force, 1865 ; the 1st (Prince Albert Victor's Own) Regt. of Punjab Cavalry, 1890 ; the 1st (Prince Albert Victor's Own) Punjab Cavalry, 1901 ; the 21st Prince Albert Victor's Own Cavalry (Frontier Force), 1903 ; present designation, 1904.
"Delhi, 1857" "Lucknow" "Ahmad Khel" "Afghanistan, 1878-80."

Field Army—Depot, Rawalpindi.

Composition—1½ Squadrons of Sikhs, ½ of Dogras, 1 of Hindustani Musalmans, 1 of Pathans.
Uniform—Blue. *Facings*—Scarlet.

COLONEL—Major-General Charles S. Maclean, c.b., c.i.e., ☒.   . 6 January 1905.

1st Commn. or date of entering service.	Names and Rank.	Army rank.	Present appointment in Regiment.	Remarks.
	Commandant.			
30 Aug. 93	Johnson, Lt.-Col. J. E. B. . .	1 July 18	1 July 18	
	Squadron Commanders. (4)			
20 Jan. 97	Gunning, Bt. Lt.-Col. G. H., D.S.O.	1 Jan. 19	14 Sep. 19	2nd-in-Comd.
6 Apl. 98	Worsley, Maj. C. F. M. . .	1 Sep. 15	8 Feb. 19	Comdg. Depot.
4 May 98	Dyke, Maj. O. M. . . .	1 Sep. 15	11 Apl. 19	With 111th Mahars.
8 Jan. 01	McCudden, Maj. J. H., D.S.O.,M.C.	8 Jan. 16	14 Sep. 19	
	Squadron Officers. (9)			
5 Oct. 01	Smart, Maj. R. W. L. deB. .	5 Oct. 16	3 Mar. 04	
29 Jan. 02	Robertson, Maj. E. D. S. . .	29 Jan. 17	15 Jan. 05	Remt. Depot.
27 Jan. 02	Grace, Maj. H. G., M.C. . .	27 Jan. 19	1 Mar. 06	
5 Aug. 05	Ismay, Bt.-Maj. (temp. Lt.-Col.) H. L.	1 Jan. 18	16 Sep. 07	Comdg. Somaliland Camel Corps.
17 Aug. 07	Lewis, Capt. R. F.	1 Sep. 15	11 Nov. 08	With 25th Cav.
9 Sep. 08	Garsin, Bt.-Maj. H. A., M.C. .	1 Jan. 19	17 Nov. 09	Lv., ex I., 12 m., 1 Jan. 20.
14 Jan. 14	Dening, Capt. J. P. . . .	14 Jan. 18	10 Oct. 14	Cav., Sch., Saugor.
15 Aug. 14	Logan, Capt. A. F., M.C. . .	15 Aug. 18	25 May 16	Inspg. Offr., I. S. Troops.
9 Nov. 14	Byrne, Capt. G. R. . . .	9 Nov. 18	30 Nov. 17	Attd.
26 June 15	Stuart-William Capt. W. L. .	26 June 19	24 Oct. 19	Attd.
19 Feb. 16	Harris, Lt. H., D.C.M. . . .	19 Feb. 17	13 July 18	Attd.
29 June 16	Bevan-Petman, Lt. B. H. . .	2 July 16	29 June 16	
18 June 17	Hanmer, Lt. C. G. . . .	18 June 18	18 Nov. 17	With 42nd Cav.
12 Jan. 16	Brookes, Lt. J. R. . . .	12 Jan. 17	4 Sep. 18	Attd.
14 Nov. 16	Wooley, Lt. J. H. C. . . .	14 Nov. 17	18 Nov. 19	Attd.
31 Aug. 18	Meyer, Lt. W. R. M. . . .	31 Aug. 19	4 Sep. 18	Attd. With 20 Horse.
21 Aug. 18	Cramer, Lt. J. M. C. . . .	21 Aug. 19	17 Jan. 19	Attd. Lv., ex I., 4 m., 18 Dec. 19.
15 Apl. 19	Mathew, 2nd-Lt. F. A. D. L. .	15 Apl. 19	15 Apl. 19	Attd.
15 Apl. 19	Leeper, 2nd-Lt. W. C. . . .	15 Apl. 19	15 Apl. 19	Attd.
	Attached.			
30 Aug. 06	Watson, Bt.-Maj. T. N., M.C. .	3 June 18	5 Dec. 19	12th Cav.
5 May 15	Stewart, Capt. I.	5 May 19	1 Aug. 18	I. A. (on probn.).
25 Sep. 16	Maxwell, Lt. H. B. . . .	25 Sep. 17	4 May 17	I. A. R. O.—Lt., ex I., m.c., 6 m.
18 June 17	Herbert, Lt. H. A. . . .	18 June 18	4 Dec. 19	26 Cav.— Lv., ex I., 8 m.,4 Feb. 20.
21 Dec. 17	Ffolkes, Lt. F. J. P. B. . .	21 Dec. 18	22 May 19	11th Lrs.
1 Feb. 18	Ferguson, Lt. J. M. . . .	1 Feb. 19	22 May 19	11th Lrs.
24 Apl. 18	Gomer, Lt. L. W. . . .	24 Apl. 19	31 Oct. 19	4th Cav.
31 Aug. 18	Ruttledge, 2nd-Lt. R. F. . .	31 Aug. 18	18 Nov. 19	34th Horse.
18 Sep. 18	Albert, 2nd-Lt. E. F. . . .	18 Sep. 18	. . . .	I. A. R. O.
15 Apl. 19	Clemons, 2nd-Lt. R. S. . .	15 Apl. 19	31 Oct. 19	4th Cav.
29 Jan. 20	Knowles, 2nd-Lt. G. . . .	29 Jan. 20	. . . .	I. A., u. l.

Risaldar-Major.

		Jemadar.	Ressaidar.	Risaldar.	Risaldar-Maj.
19 July 98	Sundar Singh, M.C. (53, 56, 71)	19 July 98	8 Apl. 02	17 Nov. 12	7 Mar. 17.

Risaldars.

		Jemadar.	Ressaidar.	Risaldar.	
6 Jan. 99	Ali Sher Khan, I.D.S.M. . . .	16 Oct. 10	21 Dec. 14	14 July 16	With 42nd Cav.
29 Dec. 94	Latif Khan (53, 56) . . .	1 Feb. 08	1 Apl. 13	10 Sep. 16	
25 Feb. 92	Mahbub Khan *Bahadur* (45a) .	10 May 10	1 July 14	14 Feb. 17	*Order of Br. I., 2nd Cl.*
21 Mar. 94	Narayan Singh *Bahadur* (53, 56, 66a).	1 July 10	11 Oct. 14	15 Sep. 17	*Order of Br. I., 2nd Cl.*
2 Dec. 98	Farzand Ali, I.D.S.M. . . .	1 July 14	14 Feb. 17	28 June 18	
18 Apl. 04	Jahangir Beg, I.O.M. . . .	4 July 15	1 Apl. 17	5 Aug. 18	
17 Apl. 94	Arbela Singh	11 Aug. 12	15 Sep. 17	3 Sep. 18	
16 Mar. 04	Muhammad Hushum (56, 66a). .	1 Apl. 10	15 May 16	14 Jan. 20.	

Figure 15 Entry from an *Indian Army List* showing J. H. McCudden DSO, MC

Promoted to Brevet Lt Colonel in 1925 and substantive Colonel in 1927, Lt Colonel J. H. McCudden DSO, MC retired on 31 January 1931. According to a letter in private hands Lt Colonel McCudden did not enjoy a long retirement as he died of a heart attack whilst out riding.

All of the information about Lt Col McCudden came from his papers in L/MIL/9 at the British Library, the Indian and British *Army Lists*, the *London Gazette*, WO 100 and some private correspondence.

6 Records of service of the Royal Flying Corps and Royal Air Force

6.1 Introduction

The Royal Flying Corps was formed in May 1912 from the Royal Engineers Balloon Section. As a corps of the British Army, the RFC played an important part in the First World War, bringing the use of aircraft from an experimental part of the army to the forefront of military strategy. The RFC and the naval equivalent, the Royal Naval Air Service, were eventually joined together to form the Royal Air Force, which was created on 1 April 1918.

As the RFC was a corps of the British Army, so the records of service of these men should be discussed briefly here. However, the RFC and RAF and all of the records which may be of interest to family historians, are more fully explained in *Air Force Records for Family Historians* by William Spencer (2000).

6.2 RFC and RAF officers

RFC and RAF officers are already mentioned in basic terms in section **2.6.5**. To find an RFC officer's file it is necessary to follow the advice laid down in **Chapter 2**. The records of RAF officers preserved in AIR 76 are arranged in alphabetical order and concern only those officers who had left the RAF by early 1920. The records are very brief and only contain basic biographical data and details of the units in which an individual served.

Unit records concerning the RFC and RAF can be found in the record series AIR 1. At the beginning of the AIR 1 catalogue there is a list of units each with a list of relevant sections within AIR 1 where records may be found. Many of these records include details of officers' services, biographical information and reports concerning their ability.

6.3 RFC other ranks

Records of service of RFC airmen can be found in the record series WO 363 and WO 364. See **Chapter 3** for further information. However, the RFC records in these series only concern men discharged prior to the formation of the RAF on 1 April 1918.

Information concerning the first 1,500 other ranks who joined the RFC can be found in *A Contemptible Little Flying Corps* by I. McInnes and J. V. Webb (1991).

An example of an early RFC record of service can be seen in **Fig 16**.

6.4 RAF other ranks

Records of men of the RFC who were still serving when it was formed into the RAF, and of those who joined the RAF from 1 April 1918 onwards, can be found in the record series AIR 79. This record series is arranged in service number order. A nominal index which provides the service numbers necessary to use AIR 79, can be found in AIR 78, which is available on microfilm in the PRO Microfilm Reading Room.

The records in AIR 79 provide basic biographical data including date and place of birth, physical description, date of enlistment, units served in and medals awarded. It is also possible to find some information concerning RFC and RAF other ranks in AIR I.

A list (Muster) of all those men serving in the RAF at the time of its formation can be found in AIR 1/819 and AIR 10/237. This muster is arranged in service number order.

6.5 Women's Royal Air Force

There are no records of Women's Royal Air Force (WRAF) officers; they were destroyed a number of years ago.

A small collection of WRAF records are preserved in the record series AIR 80. These records, arranged in alphabetical order, provide basic biographical data, the trade a woman served as and the units she served in.

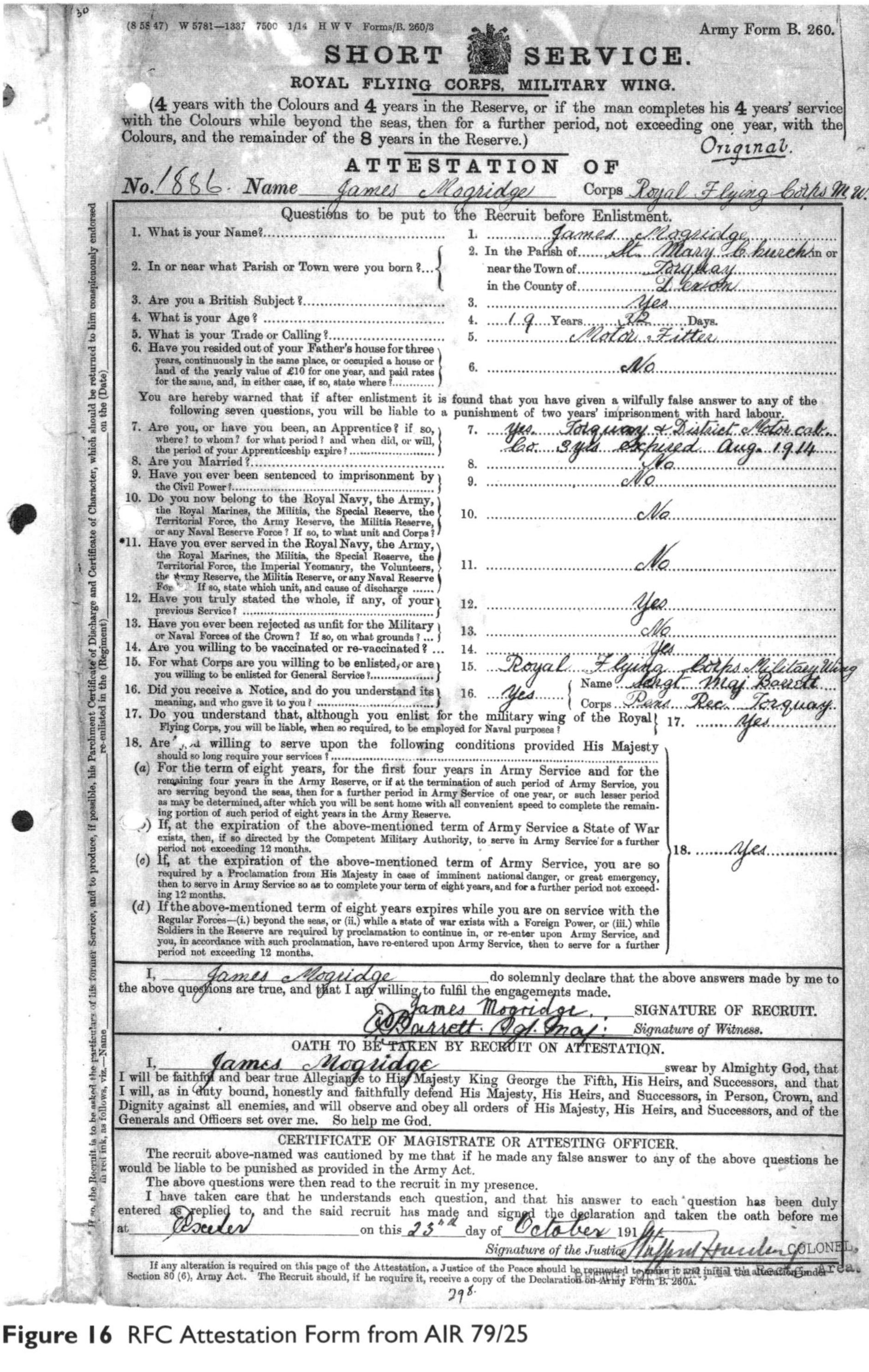

(8 58 47) W 5781—1337 7500 1/14 H W V Forms/B. 260/3

Army Form B. 260.

SHORT SERVICE.

ROYAL FLYING CORPS, MILITARY WING.

(**4** years with the Colours and **4** years in the Reserve, or if the man completes his **4** years' service with the Colours while beyond the seas, then for a further period, not exceeding one year, with the Colours, and the remainder of the **8** years in the Reserve.)

Original.

ATTESTATION OF

No. 1886. Name James Mogridge Corps Royal Flying Corps M.W.

Questions to be put to the Recruit before Enlistment.

1. What is your Name? — 1. James Mogridge
2. In or near what Parish or Town were you born? — 2. In the Parish of St. Mary Church in or near the Town of Torquay in the County of Devon
3. Are you a British Subject? — 3. Yes
4. What is your Age? — 4. 19 Years 32 Days.
5. What is your Trade or Calling? — 5. Motor Fitter
6. Have you resided out of your Father's house for three years, continuously in the same place, or occupied a house or land of the yearly value of £10 for one year, and paid rates for the same, and, in either case, if so, state where? — 6. No

You are hereby warned that if after enlistment it is found that you have given a wilfully false answer to any of the following seven questions, you will be liable to a punishment of two years' imprisonment with hard labour.

7. Are you, or have you been, an Apprentice? if so, where? to whom? for what period? and when did, or will, the period of your Apprenticeship expire? — 7. Yes. Torquay & District Motor cab Co. 3 yrs Expired Aug. 1914
8. Are you Married? — 8. No
9. Have you ever been sentenced to imprisonment by the Civil Power? — 9. No
10. Do you now belong to the Royal Navy, the Army, the Royal Marines, the Militia, the Special Reserve, the Territorial Force, the Army Reserve, the Militia Reserve, or any Naval Reserve Force? If so, to what unit and Corps? — 10. No
*11. Have you ever served in the Royal Navy, the Army, the Royal Marines, the Militia, the Special Reserve, the Territorial Force, the Imperial Yeomanry, the Volunteers, the Army Reserve, the Militia Reserve, or any Naval Reserve Force? If so, state which unit, and cause of discharge — 11. No
12. Have you truly stated the whole, if any, of your previous Service? — 12. Yes
13. Have you ever been rejected as unfit for the Military or Naval Forces of the Crown? If so, on what grounds? — 13. No
14. Are you willing to be vaccinated or re-vaccinated? — 14. Yes
15. For what Corps are you willing to be enlisted, or are you willing to be enlisted for General Service? — 15. Royal Flying Corps Military Wing
16. Did you receive a Notice, and do you understand its meaning, and who gave it to you? — 16. Yes Name Sergt Maj Barrett Corps Pens Rec. Torquay.
17. Do you understand that, although you enlist for the military wing of the Royal Flying Corps, you will be liable, when so required, to be employed for Naval purposes? — 17. Yes
18. Are you willing to serve upon the following conditions provided His Majesty should so long require your services? — 18. Yes
   (a) For the term of eight years, for the first four years in Army Service and for the remaining four years in the Army Reserve, or if at the termination of such period of Army Service, you are serving beyond the seas, then for a further period in Army Service of one year, or such lesser period as may be determined, after which you will be sent home with all convenient speed to complete the remaining portion of such period of eight years in the Army Reserve.
   (b) If, at the expiration of the above-mentioned term of Army Service a State of War exists, then, if so directed by the Competent Military Authority, to serve in Army Service for a further period not exceeding 12 months.
   (c) If, at the expiration of the above-mentioned term of Army Service, you are so required by a Proclamation from His Majesty in case of imminent national danger, or great emergency, then to serve in Army Service so as to complete your term of eight years, and for a further period not exceeding 12 months.
   (d) If the above-mentioned term of eight years expires while you are on service with the Regular Forces—(i.) beyond the seas, or (ii.) while a state of war exists with a Foreign Power, or (iii.) while Soldiers in the Reserve are required by proclamation to continue in, or re-enter upon Army Service, and you, in accordance with such proclamation, have re-entered upon Army Service, then to serve for a further period not exceeding 12 months.

I, James Mogridge do solemnly declare that the above answers made by me to the above questions are true, and that I am willing to fulfil the engagements made.

James Mogridge. SIGNATURE OF RECRUIT.

E Barrett Sgt. Maj. *Signature of Witness.*

OATH TO BE TAKEN BY RECRUIT ON ATTESTATION.

I, James Mogridge swear by Almighty God, that I will be faithful and bear true Allegiance to His Majesty King George the Fifth, His Heirs, and Successors, and that I will, as in duty bound, honestly and faithfully defend His Majesty, His Heirs, and Successors, in Person, Crown, and Dignity against all enemies, and will observe and obey all orders of His Majesty, His Heirs, and Successors, and of the Generals and Officers set over me. So help me God.

CERTIFICATE OF MAGISTRATE OR ATTESTING OFFICER.

The recruit above-named was cautioned by me that if he made any false answer to any of the above questions he would be liable to be punished as provided in the Army Act.

The above questions were then read to the recruit in my presence.

I have taken care that he understands each question, and that his answer to each question has been duly entered as replied to, and the said recruit has made and signed the declaration and taken the oath before me at Exeter on this 23rd day of October 1914

Signature of the Justice [illegible] COLONEL,

If any alteration is required on this page of the Attestation, a Justice of the Peace should be requested to make it and initial the alteration under Section 80 (6), Army Act. The Recruit should, if he require it, receive a copy of the Declaration on Army Form B. 260A.

*If so, the Recruit is to be asked the particulars of his former Service, and to produce, if possible, his Parchment Certificate of Discharge and Certificate of Character, which should be returned to him conspicuously endorsed in red ink, as follows, viz.—Name ... re-enlisted in the (Regiment) on the (Date)

298

Figure 16 RFC Attestation Form from AIR 79/25

7 Unit war diaries and operational records

7.1 Introduction

Prior to the First World War, the records kept by individual units to account for their activities during operations varied according to the interests and expertise within a unit. Although the commanding officer of an operation produced periodic despatches and reports concerning the conduct of operations, it was not until the Field Service Regulations of 1907 which in Part II laid down rules instructing commanding officers of all units to keep a unit diary when on active operations, that systematic recording began. It is these unit diaries that provide a day-to-day account of what happened to, and within, a unit, and where it happened. Beyond published regimental histories and numerous personal accounts, the unit diaries are the only other records that can provide a picture of what really happened on a day-to-day basis.

7.2 Army structures

During the First World War, the British Army expanded from a small pre-war regular army into a huge fighting machine. In order to find a specific unit war diary it helps to understand how the army was arranged. The easiest way to explain the arrangement is to look at the British Expeditionary Force in France and Flanders.

At the head of the whole army overseas was the Commander in Chief (CinC), initially Sir John French but from December 1915 until the end of the war, Field Marshal Sir Douglas Haig. Below the CinC the structure was a follows:

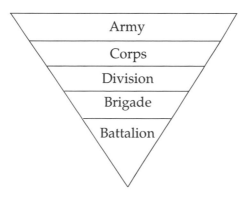

Army

Corps

Division

Brigade

Battalion

When listed, armies are usually numbered I–V, corps are also numbered using Roman numerals, divisions are listed in Arabic numerals 1–75, brigades are similarly numbered. Infantry battalions are listed using Arabic numerals, e.g. 2 Battalion or 1/4 Battalion. For more information about the numbering of regiments, see *Your Country Needs You* by Martin Middlebrook (2000).

Although the units within this chain of command could and did change, this was the hierarchy of the Army overseas. In this hierarchy there are a number of constants. Until the spring of 1918, there were always four infantry battalions in a brigade. This figure was reduced to three battalions per brigade due to manpower shortages, when many infantry battalions were disbanded and the manpower redistributed amongst other units, mostly in the same brigade if not division.

Apart from the units listed under a specific division and brigades, many units served as either army or corps troops, directly controlled by the commanders of the relevant army or corps, rather than under divisional or brigade command.

Most divisions consisted of a collection of divisional troops, answerable to and controlled directly by divisional headquarters. These troops were the artillery and other support troops (medical, supply and signals) that supported the three infantry brigades. The three infantry brigades each had their own brigade commander who was subordinate to the divisional commander but superior to each infantry battalion commander. Although a brigade could act fairly independently in minor operations, most of the time, the brigade was controlled by the divisional commander.

An infantry battalion, with a lieutenant colonel in command, was split into a number of companies, usually identified by a letter. Most battalions were split into an HQ Company and four other companies, A–D. Each company was usually commanded by a captain, although during operations where casualties were sustained command would devolve down to the next most senior individual. Each company was further broken down, firstly into platoons, commanded by a lieutenant or second lieutenant, and then into sections commanded by a sergeant or corporal.

Different parts of the army had different titles for their units. In cavalry regiments the equivalent of the infantry company was the squadron and below that the troop. Artillery was usually in brigades and then batteries. Engineers and the Army Service Corps were arranged by company.

If you know the full title of the part of the army you require a unit war diary for, you can use that title to do a keyword search on the on-line catalogue.

The arrangement of the British Expeditionary Force during the war can be found in *History of The Great War: Orders of Battle*, by A. F. Becke (1937–45). Known as the

'Orders of Battle', this work lists all units serving in either an army, corps or division. A copy of this work can be found behind the staff desk in the PRO Research Enquiries Room. The composition of the BEF at certain times during the war can also be found in the *Official History of the Great War*, a copy of which is available in the PRO Library. Orders of Battle can also be found in WO 95/5467–5487.

7.3 Unit war diaries WO 95

The diaries found in the record series WO 95 comprise over 10,000 individual unit diaries covering all operational theatres in which the British Army saw service. Diaries for dominion forces which served as part of the British Army can be found in WO 95 as can those of the Indian Army. Not only do the diaries cover operations between 1914 and 1918, they also cover operations up to 1920, including those in Russia and India.

The diaries are arranged by operational theatre and then in a hierarchical order starting at General Headquarters and then by armies, corps, divisions, brigades and then battalions. Although this is the basic chain of command, the arrangement of the catalogue can alter depending on the operational theatre.

Unit war diary operational theatres

I	France and Flanders
II	Italy
III	Gallipoli and Dardanelles
IV	Egypt, Palestine and Syria
V	Salonika, Macedonia, Turkey, Black Sea, Caucasus and South Russia
VI	Mesopotamia, Iraq and North Russia
VII	East Africa, West Africa and Cameroon
VIII	India and East Persia
IX	North Persia and Siberia
X	Colonies: Aden, Bermuda, Ceylon, Hong Kong, North China, Gibraltar Malta, Mauritius, Singapore
XI	Home Forces

If you are looking for a specific unit diary, there are a number of routes open to you to locate it.

Apart from using the printed WO 95 catalogue to find unit diaries, it is possible to locate them by doing a keyword search on the on-line catalogue. By placing the unit name in the top field of the search page and WO 95 in the last field it is possible to list all diaries for each unit. As many units saw service in more than one operational theatre and in many cases in more than one division, by using the on-line catalogue the problem of locating all of the relevant diaries is reduced.

The content of the unit war diary varies according to the level of interest that the compiler of the diary had in the task. In many cases it was the responsibility of the adjutant to compile the diary from information provided by a number of sources. In basic terms the diary should contain the location of the unit, its strength and any occurrences which the unit was either involved in or which affected it. Details of all operational action either by or against a unit and information about personnel including casualties are usually shown. Also found in most unit war diaries are operational orders from higher authority, maps and plans. Many of these are usually listed as appendixes at the end of each month. In most diaries only officers are mentioned by name, but depending upon the interest shown by the compiler other ranks may be mentioned.

Examples of typical data found in a unit war diary can be seen in **Fig 17**.

Unit war diaries can provide useful contextual information about operations, especially concerning honours and awards granted for deeds performed during those operations.

Unit War Diaries for the 63rd (Royal Naval) Division can be found in WO 95 and also in ADM 137/3063–3088.

7.4 Military Headquarters papers and correspondence WO 158

Arranged by operational theatre and then by unit down to brigade level, these records are the papers created by various units and describe in more detail than most unit war diaries numerous operations undertaken during the war. Although individuals are sometimes mentioned, especially in those papers for operational theatres other than France and Flanders, the majority of information in these files concerns the conduct of operations and the planning that took place beforehand.

7.5 Intelligence summaries WO 157

Whilst not providing information about individuals, the intelligence summaries in WO 157 do provide information about who was opposing the units sending in the report, together with information about other events at the front. These summaries are arranged by operational theatre and by unit, usually no lower than brigade.

7.6 War Office registered files: general series WO 32

A number of operational reports by a number of different commanders can be found in WO 32. Many of the files concern operations in Africa but there is also a report concerning the seizure of Tsingtau, the German colony in China, in 1914.

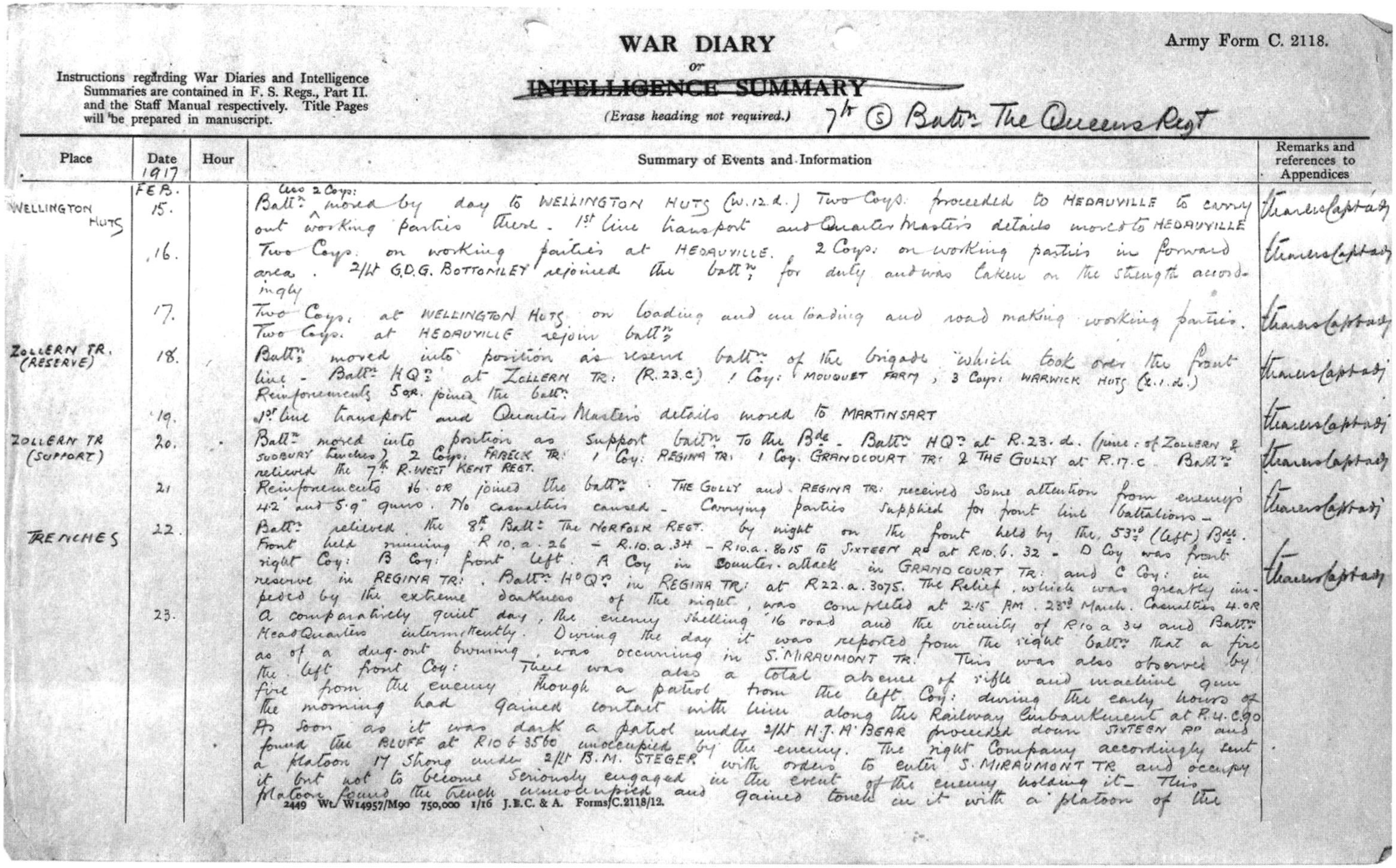

Instructions regarding War Diaries and Intelligence Summaries are contained in F. S. Regs., Part II. and the Staff Manual respectively. Title Pages will be prepared in manuscript.

WAR DIARY

or

~~INTELLIGENCE SUMMARY~~

(Erase heading not required.) 7th (S) Battn. The Queens Regt

Army Form C. 2118.

Place	Date 1917	Hour	Summary of Events and Information	Remarks and references to Appendices
WELLINGTON HUTS	FEB. 15.		Battn. less 2 Coys: moved by day to WELLINGTON HUTS (W.12.d.) Two Coys. proceeded to HEDAUVILLE to carry out working parties there. 1st line transport and Quarter Master's details moved to HEDAUVILLE	[illegible] Capt Adj
	16.		Two Coys: on working parties at HEDAUVILLE. 2 Coys: on working parties in forward area. 2/Lt G.D.G. BOTTOMLEY rejoined the battn: for duty and was taken on the strength accordingly	[illegible] Capt Adj
	17.		Two Coys: at WELLINGTON HUTS on loading and unloading and road making working parties. Two Coys. at HEDAUVILLE rejoin battn.	[illegible] Capt Adj
ZOLLERN TR. (RESERVE)	18.		Battn: moved into position as reserve battn: of the brigade which took over the front line - Battn: HQ: at ZOLLERN TR: (R.23.c) 1 Coy: MOUQUET FARM, 3 Coys: WARWICK HUTS (R.1.d.) Reinforcements 5 OR. joined the battn:	[illegible] Capt Adj
	19.		1st line transport and Quarter Master's details moved to MARTINSART	[illegible] Capt Adj
ZOLLERN TR (SUPPORT)	20.		Battn: moved into position as support battn: to the Bde. Battn: HQ: at R.23.d. (junc: of ZOLLERN & SUDBURY trenches) 2 Coys. FABECK TR: 1 Coy: REGINA TR: 1 Coy. GRANDCOURT TR: & THE GULLY at R.17.c. Battn: relieved the 7th R. WEST KENT REGT.	[illegible] Capt Adj
	21		Reinforcements 16 OR joined the battn: THE GULLY and REGINA TR: received some attention from enemy's 4.2" and 5.9" guns. No casualties caused. Carrying parties supplied for front line battalions.	[illegible] Capt Adj
TRENCHES	22.		Battn: relieved the 8th Battn: The NORFOLK REGT. by night on the front held by the 53rd (left) Bde. Front held running R10.a.26 - R.10.a.34 - R10.a.8015 to SIXTEEN Rd at R10.b.32 - D Coy was front right Coy: B Coy: front left. A Coy in counter-attack in GRANDCOURT TR: and C Coy: in reserve in REGINA TR: Battn: HQ: in REGINA TR: at R22.a.3075. The Relief, which was greatly impeded by the extreme darkness of the night, was completed at 2.15 AM. 23rd March. Casualties 4 OR	[illegible] Capt Adj
	23.		A comparatively quiet day, the enemy shelling 16 road and the vicinity of R10a 34 and Battn: Head Quarters intermittently. During the day it was reported from the right battn: that a fire as of a dug-out burning, was occurring in S. MIRAUMONT TR. This was also observed by the left front Coy: There was also a total absence of rifle and machine gun fire from the enemy though a patrol from the left Coy: during the early hours of the morning had gained contact with him along the Railway Embankment at R.4.c.90. As soon as it was dark a patrol under 2/Lt H.J.M. BEAR proceeded down SIXTEEN Rd and found the BLUFF at R10 b 3560 unoccupied by the enemy. The right Company accordingly sent a platoon 17 strong under 2/Lt B.M. STEGER with orders to enter S. MIRAUMONT TR and occupy it but not to become seriously engaged in the event of the enemy holding it. This platoon found the trench unoccupied and gained touch in it with a platoon of the	

2449 Wt. W14957/M90 750,000 1/16 J.B.C. & A. Forms/C.2118/12.

Figure 17 Unit War Diary for 7 Battalion Queen's Royal West Surrey Regiment (WO 95/2051)

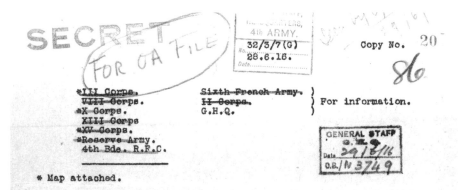

SECRET

(FOR OA FILE)

HEADQUARTERS,
4th ARMY.
No. 32/3/7 (G)
Date 28.6.16.

Copy No.   20

86

*III Corps.
VIII Corps.
*X Corps.
XIII Corps
*XV Corps.
*Reserve Army.
4th Bde. R.F.C.

Sixth French Army.)
II Corps.   )   For information.
G.H.Q.   )

GENERAL STAFF
Date 29/5/16
O.B./N 3749

* Map attached.

With reference to Fourth Army No. 32/3 (G) and No.32/3/1 (G) of 22nd June.

1.   It has been decided that if the enemy's resistence breaks down during the first phase of the operations the nearest available infantry will be pushed forward in advance of the cavalry, so that no time may be lost in pushing forward troops after an initial success.

2.   This does not involve any change in the disposition of troops at Zero on "Z" day, or in the general plan as outlined in para. 1 of Fourth Army No. 32/3 G. of 22nd June, but necessitates the III and X Corps being ready to push their reserve divisions forward as soon as it is ascertained that the enemy's resistance is broken down.
      The Cavalry of the Reserve Army will/remain in their places of assembly until these Divisions have moved forward and cleared the line of advance for the Cavalry.

3.   The Reserve Divisions of the above Corps will be directed as follows :-

         X Corps (49th) on PYS and IRLES.
         III Corps (19th) on LE SARS.

      On passing the hostile second line the above two Divisions will come under the command of the G.O.C. Reserve Army, whose H.Q. will be established at ALBERT immediately the advance is ordered by the Fourth Army.
      The X and III Corps will continue to administer their two Reserve Divisions.

4.   During their advance the flanks of the Reserve Divisions of the III and X Corps must be adequately guarded, and, in order to assist in this, the XV Corps will hold its Reserve Division in readiness to advance on the right of the Reserve Division of the III Corps.
      It should be directed on BAZENTIN - le - PETIT and High Wood, and, assisted by the remainder of the XV Corps and by the XIII Corps, will protect the right flank of the advancing troops of the Reserve Army.

5.   The VIII Corps will assist in the protection of the left flank of the Reserve Division of the X Corps by the seizure of MIRAUMONT and the SERRE - BEAUREGARD DOVECOTE Spur.

6.   III and X Corps will be ready to advance the remainder of their troops in support of their Reserve Divisions as soon as the necessary preparations can be made.

7.   When the orders for the advance of the Cavalry from their positions of assembly are issued by the Reserve Army, the

Figure 18 Military Headquarters papers (WO 158/234)

7.7 War diary extracts in WO 154

A number of items of a sensitive nature were removed from the diaries in WO 95. These extracts mostly concern disciplinary matters. WO 154 is arranged by unit.

7.8 Printed sources

Many of the operational records discussed in this chapter were used by the Cabinet Historical Section to produce the *Official History*. Written after the war, many of the volumes of the *Official History* were not published until the 1940s. Some volumes were only produced in draft and were therefore never published. The volumes of the *Official History* that were published are available in the PRO Library. Arranged by operational theatre, these histories can provide much useful information about the various battles fought around the world. Included in these histories are numerous maps.

Although not based solely on primary sources, the *Battleground Europe* series of books published by Leo Cooper are an excellent source of contextual information for the battles each volume covers. Many of these guides include illustrations of the areas they cover, including contemporary and modern photographs.

The *British Battalion* series of books by Ray Westlake and published by Leo Cooper provide a very useful synopsis of the war diaries of those infantry regiments that took part in operations in France and Belgium in 1914 and the first half of 1915, at Gallipoli or on the Somme in 1916.

7.9 Embarkation and disembarkation records (who went when)

From information contained on the Medal Index Cards (see section **9.3**), it is possible to know when an individual first sailed for service overseas. By using the date and applying it to a number of different sources, it is possible to identify the unit(s) which left Britain on that date.

The embarkation and disembarkation records list those units which sailed from or to Britain on specific dates, together with the number of men of a given unit leaving or returning. They can be found in WO 25/3533–3586 (leaving) and WO 25/3696–3746 (returning).

Two other records which provide the dates when units sailed overseas can be found in WO 379/16 and WO 162/7.

The D.A.A.Q.M.G.
British Expeditionary Force.

War Diary
_____

(a) The Battalion advanced from its base at LAO-SHAN BAY on 25/9/14.

(b) The weather at times was wet and objectionable but it did not materially affect the work. The ground on the whole was favourable, the main difficulty met with in trench digging was drainage. This was necessary on all occasions except in the sand attack position in the river bed.

(c) From 1/10/14 to 21/10/14 2 Coys were in the front line on outposts and two in reserve — these coys changed positions in little ditch. On 26/10/14 half a coy from the 2 reserve Coys was advanced to the outpost position followed by the other half on the next day. On 31/10/14 the trenches of the Artillery evening position were occupied. On the embankment of TSINGTAU Command and the same night the 1st attack position trenches were completed. On 1/11/14 the trenches of first attack position were occupied. On No 3 communication trench.

(d) No orders except those for digging parties and No 4 venture orders were issued.

(e) The course of events consisted in digging the trenches the positions by night and in occupying the line in rear by day, thus gradually working closer to the enemy.

(f) The position and action of the enemy was the same throughout until the final assault, — i.e. he held the line of the Redoubts with his infantry trenches connecting them and was backed by the line of ILTIS, BISMARCK and MOLTKE forts.

(g) The position and action of our troops
(26) 6th November an attack and Japanese attack were seen — that is those of the Battn except that the Japanese trenches for the 3rd attack position were not far forward as ours as they were opposed by No 2 Re-doubt and we were not: our trenches were therefore under rifle & machine gun and rifle fire from No 2 Redoubt

On the night of 6th November about 9 p.m. information was received that the Japanese had advanced No 3 Redoubt and later it was reported that they had blown up No 4 Redoubt. The Battalion was then ordered to send forward a relief to the German entrenchment in front of No 3 attack position and if they were found unoccupied to occupy them. The patrol found the trenches occupied and the patrol was then ordered to carry out the ordinary programme for the day i.e. occupy the 3rd attack position with a piquet and the remainder to return to the usual bivouac. At about dawn 7/11/14 heavy hostile artillery fire was directed at our trenches: soon after Japanese infantry advancing from 2" to 3" attack positions occupied No II Redoubt. The next things observed were:—

(i) Japanese infantry in occupation of No 3 Redoubt
(ii) Japanese infantry advancing from No 2 Redoubt in the direction of the hive of forts.
(iii) Japanese infantry advancing from the direc-tion of No 2 Redoubt towards DAI-TO-TCHEN and occupying the near face of it
(iv) 30 to 40 Germans retiring from the trenches about 250 yards South of the bridge over the River HAI-PO-HO.
(v) Several hundred Japanese Infantry on top of ILTIS HILL.

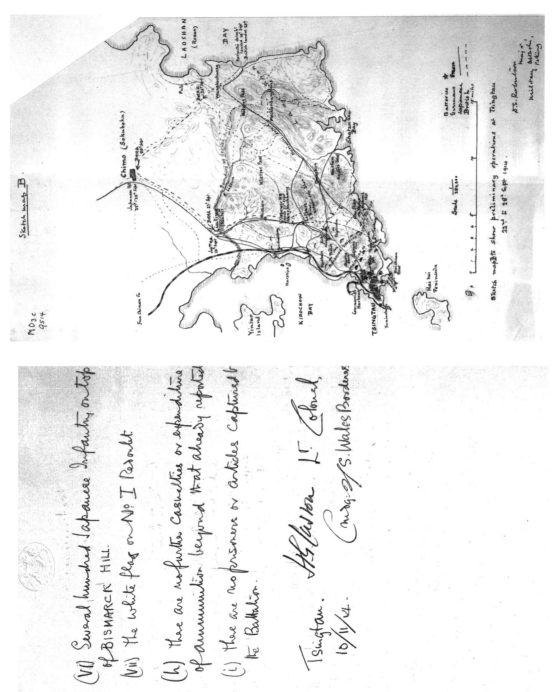

Figure 19 Report of operations leading to the capture of Tsingtau (WO 32/4996B)

The dates on which all of the infantry and cavalry regiments left the United Kingdom can be found in *British Regiments 1914–1918* by E. A. James (1993).

7.10 Army Orders

In the record series WO 123 can be found a number of different types of Administrative Orders. These Orders must not be confused with Operational Orders that can be found in WO 95 and WO 158.

Army Orders were the mechanism used to disseminate information about pay and conditions, uniforms and equipment, and honours and awards, and were sent to all British Army units around the world. These Orders for the period 1914–18 can be found in WO 123/56–60, they are internally indexed. Any announcement made in an Army Order is given a number and therefore there is only one item of information with that number in that year. In many cases items announced in Army Orders may refer to an Order from a previous year.

General Routine Orders (GROs) differ from Army Orders in as much as they are specific to a given operational theatre and the information they contain is more pertinent to the operational theatre than to the British Army as a whole.

The information contained in GROs varies from theatre to theatre. In most theatres they contain information about courts martial (the fact that one is being held, who it is to try and who will hold it, and the results of any trials, especially if the death sentence was passed), equipment and in many cases messages from high command to the whole army in a given theatre. Other information found in these Orders may vary. In the GROs for East Africa and also for Mesopotamia, information about officers' appointments, promotions and resignations may also be found.

GROs for the First World War period can be found under the following references:

Theatre	Reference
France	WO 123/199–203
Italy	WO 123/279
Egypt	WO 123/280–282
East Africa	WO 123/288–289
Mesopotamia	WO 123/290
Salonika	WO 123/293

8 Trench and other maps

8.1 Introduction

During the First World War tens of thousands of maps were produced for use at or near the front line. Many maps were based upon work carried out by Belgian or French surveyors. However, the majority of maps used during the war were produced by the survey sections of the Royal Engineers, the Geographical Section General Staff (GSGS). Although many of the maps were produced using traditional surveying methods, much of the detail added to maps during the war was based on aerial reconnaissance photographs taken by the RFC and RAF.

In the Public Record Office are preserved over 10,000 maps showing the disposition of both British and German forces in various places and at various times throughout the war.

8.2 Trench maps

The collections of trench maps preserved in the PRO are arranged by operational theatre, then by scale and then in sheet number order. The following record series contain trench maps:

- WO 297   Western Front
- WO 298   Salonika
- WO 300   German South West and German East Africa
- WO 301   Gallipoli
- WO 302   Mesopotamia
- WO 303   Palestine
- WO 369   Italy

Depending upon the date and scale, the amount of information contained on the map may vary. Although the description of each map in the catalogue will tell you its effective date and whether it shows the Allied (A) or German (G) lines, it is sometimes only possible to find a map that shows the area you may be interested in, either before or after the exact date you require.

Most of the trench maps are for the war from 1915 onwards, with most being later than that. If you are unable to find a map in one of the trench map record series, you may need to look in WO 153 or see if one is preserved in the unit war diary.

There were a variety of different scales used on maps in the First World War. However, although there are many maps of the 1:5000 scale which can be very detailed, the majority preserved in the PRO are in 1:10000 and 1:20000, which still provide enough information for most uses.

8.3 How to use trench maps

There is a brief guide to using trench maps available at the staff desks in the Research Enquiries Room and the Map and Large Document Reading Room at the PRO. It is recommended that you use this guide to find all maps in WO 297 and to work out any particular grid reference.

In basic terms each area of France and Belgium was given a number, which was further split into NW, NE, SW and SE. Each of these four sheets can be further divided into four sheets numbered 1–4. A further division by letter and then number will eventually mean that you will be able to work out any given position in a box 1,000 yards by 1,000 yards.

Index maps which tell you what number was given to a particular area are available at the beginning of the WO 297 catalogue and at the back of the 'First World War, 1914–1918: Military Maps' leaflet.

If you know the number and geographical part of a given sheet, e.g. 28 NW, you can use that data to do a keyword search on the PRO on-line catalogue.

An example of using a grid reference found in a unit war diary is shown below:

> According to the diary of 18 Division for July 1917 (WO 95/2016), the division was occupying positions shown on 1:20000 sheets 28 NW/NE. The specific grid reference where 7 Battalion Queen's Royal West Surrey Regiment were in July 1917 was I23a58.40. This translates to Sheet 28 NW 3, Box I, Box a, grid 58.40. The closest map to the date 10 July 1917, when 2/Lt/A/Captain H. J. A'Bear (see section **2.11**) was killed is WO 297/701. This map is shown in **Fig 20**.

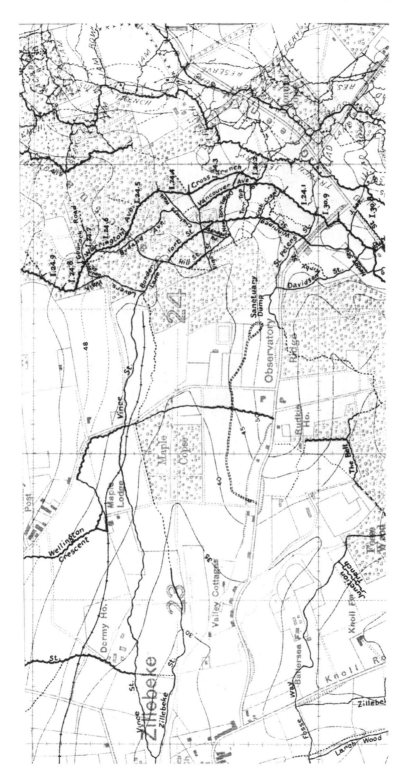

Figure 20 A detail section from a typical 1:20000 trench map (WO 297/701)

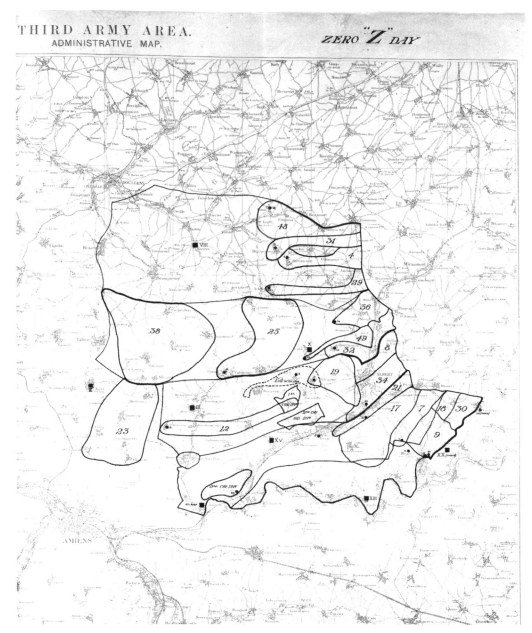

Figure 21 An example of an annotated map (WO 153/248)

8.4 Military Headquarters maps WO 153

Most trench maps were not allowed too close to the front line as the data contained on them could be of use to the enemy should the position be captured.

Detailed maps maintained by brigade, division, corps and Army Headquarters, showing dispositions of troops, enemy artillery positions, planning and progress of offensive operations are in WO 153. Many of the maps can be found using the on-line catalogue by searching using a place name, unit identity and date. As many of these maps were kept by high command, it is possible to find maps showing exact unit positions rather than working out a position from a grid reference. An example of an annotated map can be seen in **Fig 21**.

8.5 Other maps

There are a wide variety of different map record series. WO 78 is the key pre-First World War record series. Maps showing operations in West and East Africa can be found in CO 700.

9 Campaign medals

9.1 Introduction

Six different campaign medals were awarded for service during the First World War and apart from exceptional cases, the maximum number of these medals which could be awarded to one man or woman, was three. The exceptions to the rule were those individuals who served in the merchant navy, either before or in some cases after serving in the army, and who received the Mercantile Marine War Medal. This precluded recipients from receiving the Victory Medal, although many did actually receive it!

Many men and women who were discharged from the army as a result of sickness or wounds contracted or received during the war, were awarded a specific badge called the Silver War Badge. The records concerning these badges can be found with the campaign medal records. A Silver War Badge is shown on the cover of this book.

All campaign medals issued for service during the war were named, either on the back (the reverse) in the case of the two stars, or around the edge in the case of the circular medals. For other ranks the naming on all medals includes name, rank, number and regiment or corps. In the case of the 1914 Star, the naming also includes the battalion of the regiment. For officers, apart from on the 1914 Star and 1914/15 Star where the unit is given, only rank and name are given on the British War Medal and Victory Medal.

The campaign medals awarded for service during the war were issued from 1919 onwards. Medals won by other ranks were sent automatically, as were those won by individuals who were no longer living. Officers had to apply for their campaign medals which is one reason why it is possible to find the medal index card for an officer missing – he never applied.

For further information about the campaign medals awarded during the period 1914–18, see *British Battles and Medals* by E. C. Joslin, A. R. Litherland and B. T. Simpkin (1988).

9.2 The medals and Silver War Badge

The 1914 Star, authorized in 1917, was awarded to those military personnel and some civilians who saw service in France and Belgium between 5 August and 22 November 1914. In 1919 a bar with the inscription '5th Aug–22nd Nov' was sanctioned. Only those personnel who had actually been under fire during the specified dates on the bar, were eligible. This medal should always be accompanied by a British War Medal and a Victory Medal.

The 1914/15 Star, authorized in 1918, was awarded to those service personnel and civilians who saw service in France and Belgium from 23 November 1914 to 31 December 1915, and to those individuals who saw service in any other operational theatre, apart from France and Belgium, between 5 August 1914 and 31 December 1915. These other operational theatres are listed in section **9.6**, but included East and West Africa, Gallipoli and Egypt. This medal should always be accompanied by a British War Medal and a Victory Medal.

The British War Medal 1914–20, authorized in 1919, was awarded to eligible service personnel and civilians alike. Qualification for the award varied slightly depending on which service the individual was in. The basic requirement for army personnel was that they either entered a theatre of war or rendered approved service overseas between 5 August 1914 and 11 November 1918. Service in Russia between 1919 and 1920 also qualified for the award. This medal could be awarded on its own.

The Victory Medal 1914–19 was also authorized in 1919 and was awarded to those eligible personnel who served on the establishment of a unit in an operational theatre. The Victory Medal should always be accompanied by at least a British War Medal.

The Territorial Force War Medal 1914–19 was awarded to members of the Territorial Force only. To qualify for the award the recipient had to have been a member of the Territorial Force on or prior to 30 September 1914, and to have served in an operational theatre outside the United Kingdom between 5 August 1914 and 11 November 1918. Those individuals who received either a 1914 Star or 1914/15 Star, were not eligible for this award.

The Mercantile Marine War Medal, authorized in 1919, was awarded to those merchant seamen who undertook one or more voyages through areas of the sea specified as either a danger area or war zone. The medal roll for this award is separate from the War Office medal rolls for the First World War, and can be found under the reference BT 351. The roll is arranged in alphabetical order and is available on microfiche in the PRO Microfilm Reading Room.

The Silver War Badge (SWB), sometimes erroneously called the Silver Wound Badge, was authorized in September 1916 and takes the form of a circular silver badge with the legend 'For King and Empire – Services Rendered' surrounding the George V cypher. The badge was awarded to all of those military personnel who were discharged as a result of sickness or wounds contracted or received during the war, either at home or overseas. The badges are numbered on the back.

The medal rolls for all of these awards, apart from the Mercantile Marine War Medal, can be found in the record series WO 329. In order to access these rolls it is necessary to use the index, called the Medal Index Cards, which are in the record series WO 372 and which are available on microfiche in the PRO Microfilm Reading Room.

9.3 The Medal Index Cards

The Medal Index Cards (MIC) in the record series WO 372 comprise over 10,000 sheets of microfiche, each containing 360 separate index cards. These cards were created by the Army Medal Office and consist of a name index in alphabetical order with the names then placed in 'Regimental Order of Precedence'. This means for example, that if there were 200 John Smiths, they would be in a specific order which would be understood by the army, rather than in random order. There are two collections of these cards; one for men and one for women. Both collections include officers and other ranks, as well as civilians.

The name order in the index cards usually conforms to the following sequence:

Jones J
Jones James
Jones John
Jones Jonathan
Jones Julius
Jones J A
Jones J A A
Jones J B A
Jones J C

Each sheet of microfiche is arranged with the first of the 360 cards starting in the top left hand corner, with the last card being in the bottom right hand corner:

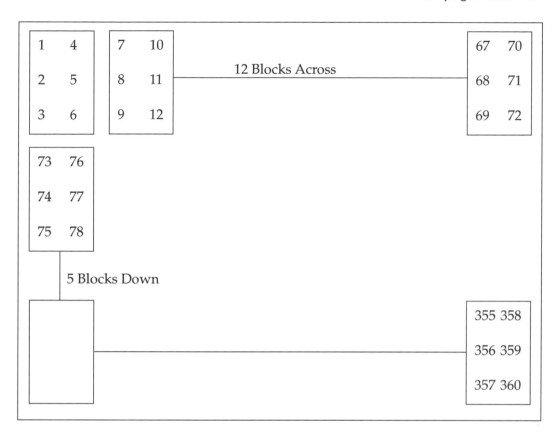

From this plan it can be seen that the first individual card is in the top left hand corner, with the next two cards below that and the next three parallel to the first three. The MICs were filmed in boxes of six, with 12 blocks across and 5 blocks down.

The original medal index cards were produced in a number of varieties. An example of a typical card can be seen in **Fig 22**. On many cards can be seen the word 'over'. On the back of about 10 per cent of the cards (mostly those for officers) was written correspondence information. This data has not been filmed.

Each Medal Index Card includes surname, initial(s) or forename(s), rank(s), number(s), regiment(s) or corps served in, the medals to which a man or woman was entitled (specifying each medal, the roll it is recorded on and the page of the roll), the first operational theatre served in, the date of entry to that theatre, and any important remarks.

Apart from the medal roll references, the unit data and the date when an individual went overseas, information found in the remarks section of the Medal Index Card can show if an individual was a prisoner of war, died of wounds or was killed in action, whether the individual was commissioned or if they transferred to the Royal Navy or Royal Air Force.

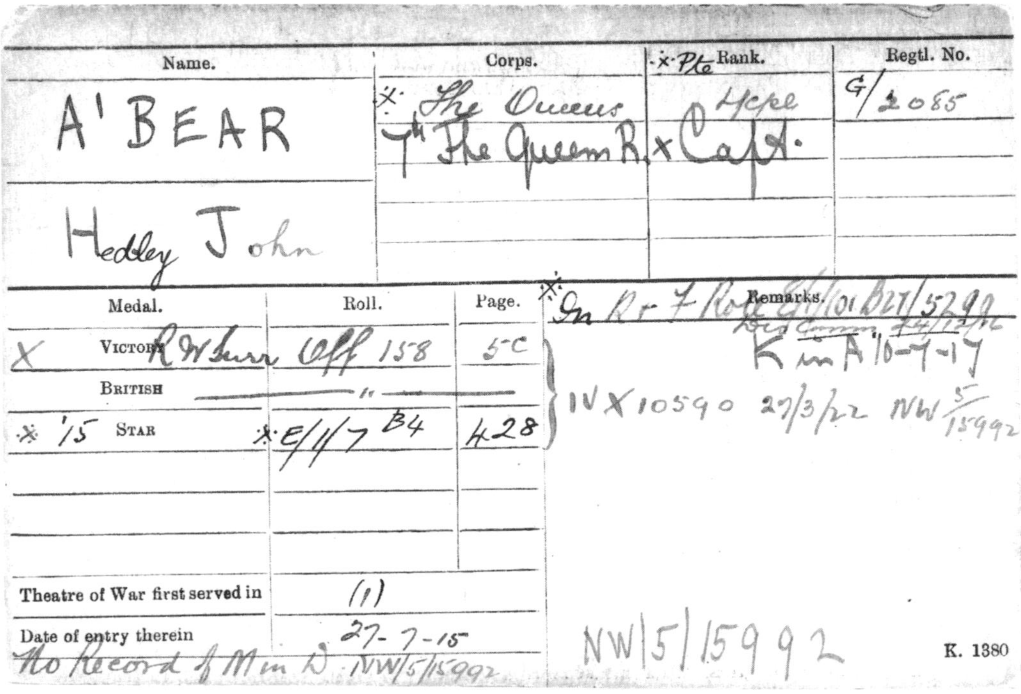
Name. Corps. Rank. Regtl. No.
A'BEAR The Queens 4cpl G/2085
7th The Queen R. Capt.
Hedley John
Medal. Roll. Page. Remarks.
VICTORY RWSurr Off 158 5C
BRITISH "
15 STAR E/4/7 B4 428
K in A 10-7-17
IVX10590 27/3/22 NW/5/15992
Theatre of War first served in (1)
Date of entry therein 27-7-15
No Record of Min D. NW/5/15992
NW/5/15992
K. 1380

Figure 22 A Medal Index Card (WO 372)

Below the list of medals an individual qualified for there may be found the term 'Clasp and Roses', which indicates that the recipient of a 1914 Star also qualified for the dated bar for their medal because they had actually seen action under fire between 5 August and 22 November 1914.

An MIC may also include information about a number of other campaign medals awarded for campaigns in Africa, India or the Middle East. Apart from the medal rolls for the Africa General Service Medal which can be found in WO 100, the PRO does not hold the medal rolls for post-war service in India or the Middle East.

Another medal that may be noted on the MIC is the award of the Territorial Efficiency Medal to members of the Territorial Army. The PRO does not hold a roll for these awards.

At the bottom of an MIC may be found the term 'EMB' or 'Emblems' and an alpha-numeric reference, which indicates that the recipient of the medals was 'Mentioned in Despatches'. See section **10.9** for further information.

In order to obtain the original medal roll, it is necessary to convert the Army Medal Office references found in the 'Roll' column and 'Page' column of the Medal Index Card into a WO 329 document reference as explained in section **9.5**.

9.4 The medal rolls

The medal rolls to which the Medal Index Cards (WO 372) are the key, can be found as original records under the reference WO 329. These medal rolls are split into a number of different rolls as follows:

- British War and Victory Medals
- 1914 Star
- 1914/15 Star
- Territorial Force War Medal
- Silver War Badge

In most cases the rolls will tell which specific unit the individual served in to qualify for the medals. This is especially so regarding the 1914 and 1914/15 Star medal rolls. The rolls of the Silver War Badge will tell you when an individual joined the army, when they were discharged and why, whether it was sickness or wounds. The SWB roll will also tell the ages of individuals on discharge and whether or not they served overseas.

9.5 How to use the medal records

The Medal Index Cards are the key to locating the correct medal roll(s) in WO 329.

Having located the correct MIC for an individual, it is necessary to consult two books before you order the medal rolls on the document ordering computer. The 'Key to the Medal Roll Index' will enable you to find the correct roll in WO 329/1. The 'Key' lists by medal where in WO 329/1 you need to look. Arranged by medal type and by other rank or officer, the 'Key' lists all of the different alphanumeric references and tells you on which page of WO 329/1 they can be found.

Arrangement of 'The Key to the Medal Roll Index'

Medal	Page
BWM and VM O/Rs	1–6
BWM and VM Off	7–13
1914 Star O/Rs	13–15
1914 Star Off	15–21
1914/15 Star O/Rs	21–4
1914/15 Star Off	24–30
TFWM O/Rs	30–33
TFWM Off	33–6
SWB All ranks	37–9

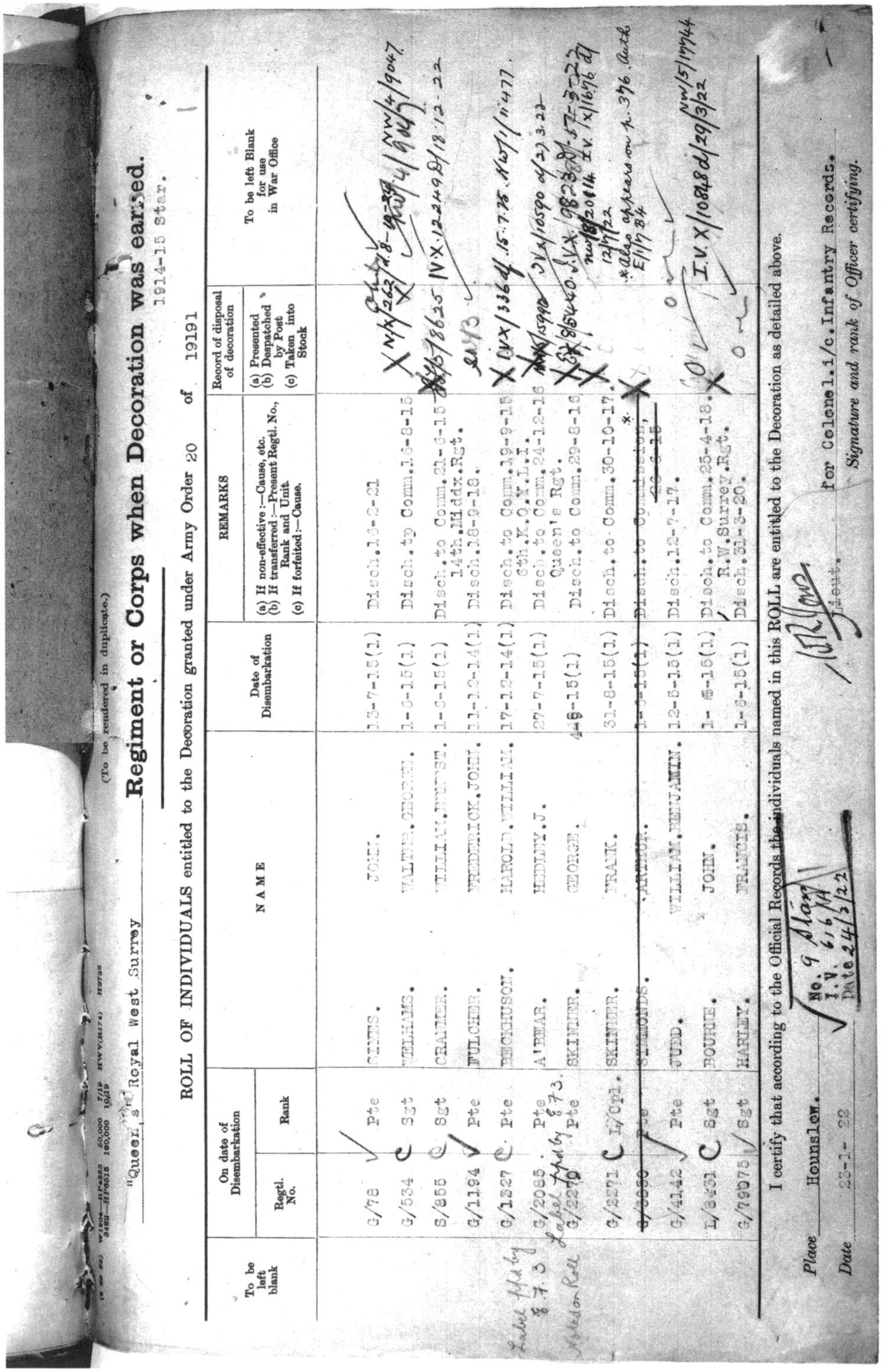
(To be rendered in duplicate.)

"Queen's" Royal West Surrey

Regiment or Corps when Decoration was earned.

1914-15 Star.

ROLL OF INDIVIDUALS entitled to the Decoration granted under Army Order 20 of 1919

To be left blank	Regtl. No.	Rank	NAME	Date of Disembarkation	REMARKS	Record of disposal of decoration	To be left Blank for use in War Office
	G/78	Pte	SIMES. JOHN.	13-7-15(1)	Disch.13-3-21		
	G/534	Sgt	WELHAMS. WALTER GEORGE.	1-6-15(1)	Disch.to Comm.16-8-15		
	S/855	Sgt	CRAMMER. WILLIAM [illegible]	1-6-15(1)	Disch.to Comm.21-6-15 14th.Middx.Rgt.		
	G/1194	Pte	FULCHER. FREDERICK JOHN.	11-12-14(1)	Disch.18-9-18.		
	G/1327	Pte	BECKHUSON. HAROLD WILLIAM.	17-12-14(1)	Disch.to Comm.19-9-15 6th.K.O.Y.L.I.		
	G/2085	Pte	A'BEAR. HEDLEY J.	27-7-15(1)	Disch.to Comm.24-12-16 Queen's Rgt.		
	G/2270	Pte	SKINNER. GEORGE.	4-8-15(1)	Disch.to Comm.29-8-16		
	G/2271	L/Cpl.	SKINNER. FRANK.	31-8-15(1)	Disch.to Comm.30-10-17.		
	G/3050	Pte	SIMMONDS. ARTHUR.	[illegible]	[illegible]		
	G/4142	Pte	JUDD. WILLIAM BENJAMIN.	12-5-15(1)	Disch.12-7-17.		
	L/8431	Sgt	BOURNE. JOHN.	1-6-15(1)	Disch.to Comm.25-4-18. R.W.Surrey Rgt.		
	G/76075	Sgt	HARLEY. FRANCIS.	1-8-15(1)	Disch.31-3-20.		

I certify that according to the Official Records the individuals named in this ROLL are entitled to the Decoration as detailed above.

Place Hounslow.

Date 25-1-22

Lieut. For Colonel i/c. Infantry Records.

Signature and rank of Officer certifying.

Figure 23 A WO 329 medal roll (WO 329/2614)

Once you have located the relevant page, you need to see which page of the medal roll can be found in which WO 329 reference. Many of the medal rolls run to several thousands of pages. The correct WO 329 reference for a given medal roll is given on the right hand side of the page in WO 329/1.

9.5.1. Using H. J. A'Bear as an example

Taking the 1914/15 Star which was qualified for first, the entry under the Roll column on the MIC states 'E/1/7b4', with the page number 428. Using the 'Key to the Medal Roll Index', the 1914/15 Star medal roll with this reference is on page 238 of WO 329/1. Page 428 of the medal roll with the original reference 'E/1/7b4' can be found in WO 329/2614. The page showing H. J. A'Bear can be seen in **Fig 23**. H. J. A'Bear was commissioned in 1917. The medal roll entry for his British War Medal and Victory Medal are on Officer's Roll 158 page 5c. This roll entry is on page 10 of the 'Key' and notes that the correct reference for the medal roll is WO 329/2182.

The system of using the 'Key' and then WO 329 should help you to avoid ordering the wrong medal roll. When using the 'Key' make sure you use the correct medal section and the officer's or other rank's section as applicable.

9.6 Operational theatres of war 1914–20 – alphanumeric codes

The alphanumeric codes for each theatre of war, e.g. 1a relating to France and Belgium, are also used in the records of service. For those personnel who first saw operational service before 31 December 1915 and who therefore received either a 1914 Star or 1914/15 Star, as well as the British War and Victory Medals, the codes used differ slightly from those used for personnel who only saw their first operational service from 1 January 1916 onwards.

To 31/12/1915	From 1/1/1916

1	1 Western Europe
	    a France and Belgium
	    b Italy

2	2 Balkans
	    a Greek Macedonia, Serbia, Bulgaria and
	       European Turkey
	    b Gallipoli (Dardanelles)

	3 Russia (4/5 August 1914 – 1/2 July 1920)
3	4 Egypt

a 4/5 November 1914 – 18/19 March 1916
b 18/19 March 1916 – 31 October/
1 November 1918

4   5 Africa
a East Africa, Nyasaland and Northern
Rhodesia
b South West Africa
c Cameroon
d Nigeria
e Togoland

5   6 Asia
a Hedjaz
b Mesopotamia
c Persia
d Trans Caspia
e South West Arabia
f Aden
g Frontier regions of India
h Tsingtau

6   7 Australasia
a New Britain
b New Ireland
c Kaiser Wilhelmland
d Admiralty Islands
e Nauru
f German Samoa

9.7 The regimental order of precedence

The regimental order of precedence is based on the date specific units were originally founded. The number at the end of each infantry regiment, starting with the Royal Scots, is the original numerical identity of the unit prior to 1881 and is the number used to identify the regiment in the officers index in WO 338, to denote which regiment an officer was first commissioned into. See section **2.3** for further details.

1 Life Guards	Royal Horse Artillery
2 Life Guards	1 Dragoon Guards
Royal Horse Guards	2 Dragoon Guards
Household Battalion	3 Dragoon Guards

4 Dragoon Guards
5 Dragoon Guards
6 Dragoon Guards
7 Dragoon Guards
1 Dragoons
2 Dragoons
6 Dragoons
5 Lancers
9 Lancers
12 Lancers
16 Lancers
21 Lancers
The Yeomanry Regts
Royal Artillery
Royal Field Artillery
Royal Engineers
Royal Flying Corps
Grenadier Guards
Coldstream Guards
Scots Guards
Irish Guards
Welsh Guards
Royal Scots **1**
Queen's (Royal West Surrey)
    Regt **2**
Buffs (East Kent) Regt **3**
King's Own Regt **4**
Northumberland Fusiliers **5**
Royal Warwickshire Regt **6**
Royal Fusiliers **7**
The King's (Liverpool) Regt **8**
Norfolk Regt **9**
Lincolnshire Regt **10**
Devon Regt **11**
Suffolk Regt **12**
Somerset Light Infantry **13**
Prince of Wales's Own (West Yorks)
    Regt **14**
East Yorkshire Regt **15**
Bedford Regt **16**
Leicester Regt **17**
Royal Irish Regt **18**
Yorkshire Regt **19**

Lancashire Fusiliers **20**
Royal Scots Fusiliers **21**
Cheshire Regt **22**
Royal Welch Fusiliers **23**
South Wales Borderers **24**
King's Own Scottish Borderers **25**
Cameronians (Scottish Rifles) **26**
Royal Inniskilling Fusiliers **27**
Gloucester Regt **28**
Worcester Regt **29**
East Lancashire Regt **30**
East Surrey Regt **31**
Duke of Cornwall's Light Infantry **32**
Duke of Wellington's (West Riding)
    Regt **33**
Border Regt **34**
Royal Sussex Regt **35**
Hampshire Regt **37**
South Staffordshire Regt **38**
Dorset Regt **39**
Prince of Wales's Volunteers (South Lancs)
    Regt **40**
Welsh Regt **41**
Black Watch (Royal Highlanders) **42**
Oxfordshire and Buckinghamshire Light
    Infantry **43**
Essex Regt **44**
Notts and Derby (Sherwood
    Foresters) Regt **45**
Loyal North Lancashire Regt **47**
Northamptonshire Regt **48**
Princess Charlotte of Wales's
    (Royal Berkshire) Regt **49**
Queen's Own (Royal West
    Kent) Regt **50**
King's Own Yorkshire Light
    Infantry **53**
Shropshire Light Infantry **53**
Duke of Cambridge's Own
    (Middlesex) Regt **57**
King's Royal Rifle Corps **60**
Duke of Edinburgh's
    (Wiltshire) Regt **62**

Manchester Regt **63**
Prince of Wales's (North Staffordshire) Regt **64**
York and Lancaster Regt **65**
Durham Light Infantry **68**
Highland Light Infantry **71**
Seaforth Highlanders **72**
Gordon Highlanders **75**
Queen's Own Cameron Highlanders **79**
Royal Irish Rifles **83**
Princess Victoria's (Royal Irish Fusiliers) **87**
Connaught Rangers **88**
Princess Louise's (Argyll and Sutherland Highlanders) **91**
Prince of Wales's Leinster Regt (Royal Canadians) **100**
Royal Munster Fusiliers **101**

Royal Dublin Fusiliers **102**
Rifle Brigade
Royal Army Chaplains Department
Army Service Corps
Royal Army Medical Corps
Army Ordnance Corps
Army Veterinary Corps
Machine Gun Corps
Royal Tank Corps
Labour Corps
Honourable Artillery Company
Monmouthshire Regt
Cambridgeshire Regt
London Regt
Hertfordshire Regt
Northern Cyclist Battalion
Highland Cyclist Battalion
Kent Cyclist Battalion
Huntingdon Cyclist Battalion

This regimental order of precedence is based on a number of different sources. To find the order of precedence of all regiments and corps during the war, especially as a number of new units were created between 1914 and 1918, see the *Army List*.

10 Awards for gallantry and meritorious service

10.1 Introduction

Over 300,000 awards for gallantry or meritorious service were bestowed upon men and women of the British armed forces during the First World War. From the Victoria Cross to a Mentioned in Despatches, it is possible to find at least the date when the award was announced in the *London Gazette*. In many cases it is possible to find out exactly what an individual did to win an award, and in some cases, even when and where the deed was performed.

A number of awards were granted to non-British nationals, i.e. those who were not members of the British Empire. As such these awards were not announced in the *London Gazette* but in numerous cases it is possible to find some mention of them amongst the records of the Foreign Office and War Office.

Many awards announced in the *London Gazette* were accompanied by a citation. The citation was the brief note which described the deed for which the award being announced was won. In many cases the citation was published some time after the award was announced in the *London Gazette*. For further information about this and other aspects of the *London Gazette* see section **10.2**.

Information concerning the institution of gallantry awards can be found in WO 32 Codes 50–52 and in *British Gallantry Awards* by P. E. Abbott and J. M. A. Tamplin (1981).

10.2 The *London Gazette*

The *London Gazette* is an official newspaper of the state and has been in existence since 1665. Information found in the *London Gazette* includes commissions and announcements concerning honours and awards. The *London Gazette* is preserved in the Public Record Office in the record series ZJ 1. The indexes for the period 1914–20 are available on the open shelves in the Microfilm Reading Room. All of the *London Gazettes* for the period 1914–20 are available on microfilm in the Microfilm Reading Room.

To find an award in the *London Gazette* it is first necessary to consult the relevant *Gazette* index. Each index covers a three-month period, that published in March also

68   INDEX TO THE LONDON GAZETTE.   [Vol. II, 1917.

STATE INTELLIGENCE.

R

Railway and Canal Traffic Act, 1888, amendment of classification 4356

Recorders:
Carmarthen Borough, Roland Edmund Lomax Vaughan Williams, K.C. 5884
Merthyr Tydfil, Borough of, Edward William Milner-Jones 5515

Regina, Saskatchewan, Jesse H. Johnson, Consul of U.S.A. at... 6180

Registrar-General in England, Birth and Deaths Registration Act, 1874, orders as to sub-districts:
Amesbury 3975
Blockley 6190
Chard 5644
Crewkerne 5644
Halford 6190
Ilminster 5644
London City 3615
Shipston-on-Stour 6190

Rhodesia, Louis Marie Frédéric Henri Rodde, Consul-General of France for 6180

442, Romford-road, Forest Gate, E. Auxiliary L.C.C. Home, temporary certificate 6410

Royal Commission on Paper, new Commission and extension of terms of reference 5513

Royal Commission on Sugar Supply, Member, Sir Joseph White-Todd, Bart., appointed ... 3954

Royal Company of Archers. (See George V., Bodyguard for Scotland) 6182

Royal Patriotic Fund Corporation, Statutory Committee:
Chairman, Rt. Hon. George Nicoll Barnes appointed ... 5222
Member, Sir Arthur Sackville Trevor Griffith-Boscawen, appointed 5222

Royal Red Cross:
First Class:
Allen, Miss G. M. 5487
Davidge, Miss H. 5487
Forrest, Miss A. McI. ... 5487
Fox, Miss E. C. 5487
Greig, Superintending Sister Miss Flora Tindal ... 5462
Holmes, Miss F. R. 5487
Humphreys, Miss E. C. ... 5487
Jones, Miss K. Conway ... 5866
—— Miss M. 5487
Luckes, Miss Eva C. E. ... 4294
Lumsden, Miss R. E. ... 5487
Lyde, Miss E. M. 5487
Martin, Miss M. L. 5487
Matheson, Miss J. 5487
Minns, Miss E. J. 5487
Mowat, Miss A. C. 5487
Niven, Miss L. 5487
O'Curran, Miss P. A. ... 5487
Phillips, Mrs. E. H. ... 5487
Rice, Miss F. M. 5487
Smales, Miss J. 5487
Smith, Miss M. 5487
Taylor, Miss A. 5487
Wood, Miss L. B. 5487

Second Class:
Aitkin, Miss M. M. 5487
Allan, Miss A. D. (Sister) (correction) 4597
Allen, Miss F. M. L. ... 5487
Arthur, Miss G. J. 5487
Ashlin-Thomas, Miss M. ... 5487
Aukett, Miss H. 5487
Baldrey, Miss E. E. ... 5487
Barker, Miss E. 5487
Blackburn, Miss E. ... 5487
Blyth, Miss J. W. 5487
Boulton, Sister Miss Fanny ... 5866
Brock, Miss L. 5487

Royal Red Cross (cont.):
Second Class (cont.):
Buckham, Miss J. B. ... 5487
Carter, Miss J. E. 5487
Casserley, Miss A. E. ... 5487
Clark, Miss E. S. 5487
Coombe, Miss E. F. ... 5487
Coupar, Miss M. 5487
Custance, Miss G. E. ... 5487
Early, Miss M. A. 5487
Esden, Miss A. H. 5487
Evers, Miss W. A. 5487
Fisher, Miss K. 5487
Fitzgerald, Miss A. L. F. ... 5487
Foley, Miss M. G. 5487
Gamble, Miss L. A. 5488
Gardiner, Miss S. S. ... 5487
Graham, Miss H. 5488
Grant, Miss D. E. 5488
Grieg, Miss M. 5487
Griffith, Miss P. M. ... 5488
Heggie, Miss M. B. 5488
Heinrich, Miss H. F. ... 5488
Howe, Miss G. A. 5488
Jamieson, Miss M. C. ... 5488
Jones, Miss C. W. 5488
Kelly, Miss L. G. 5488
Linton, Miss W. 5488
Little, Miss K. 5488
Litton, Miss G. E. 5488
Loughton, Miss M. McL. ... 5488
Lyle, Miss E. M. 5488
McBeth, Miss M. 5488
McCullough, Miss G. B. ... 5488
McEachern, Miss L. ... 5488
McGeorge, Miss J. 5488
Mackenzie, Miss M. 5488
Martin, Miss E. 5488
Mead, Miss Alice 4294
Miller, Miss G. 5488
Mole, Miss Marion 4294
Morris, Miss J. M. 5488
Morrison, Miss M. E. ... 5488
Newcome, Miss A. 5488
Newman, Miss M. C. E. ... 5488
Niccol, Miss J. S. H. ... 5488
Nicoll, Mrs. M. 5488
O'Brien, Miss M. 5488
O'Dwyer, Miss I. 5488
Passmore, Sister Miss Edith ... 5866
Phillips, Miss A. M. ... 5488
Rapson, Miss F. H. ... 5488
Robinson, Miss C. M. ... 5488
Ryder, Miss H. 5488
Smith, Miss M. 5488
Spittall, Miss J. 5488
Spratt, Mrs. F. 5488
Stapledon, Mrs. N. 5488
Storey, Miss M. P. 5488
Strange, Miss C. E. 5488
Tait, Miss H. E. 5488
Taylor, Miss A. M. B. ... 5488
Tucker, Miss E. J. 5488
Wessels, Miss E. S. 5488
White, Miss R. 5488
Wilson, Miss C. W. 5488
—— Miss D. 5488
Wood, Miss M. 5488
Wyllie, Miss A. 5488

Royal Victorian Order:
Royal Victorian Chain:
Rosebery, Archibald Philip, Earl of, K.G., K.T., P.C. ... 5462
Knights Grand Cross:
Beatty, Admiral Sir David, G.C.B., K.C.V.O., D.S.O. ... 6409
Hamilton, Admiral Sir Frederick Tower, K.C.B., C.V.O. ... 6409
Hopwood, the Rt. Hon. Sir Francis John Stephens, G.C.B., G.C.M.G. ... 5462
Knights Commander:
Brock, Rear-Admiral Osmond De Beauvoir, C.B., C.M.G. ... 6409
Carter, Sir Maurice Bonham, K.C.B. 5462
Pakenham, Rear-Admiral Sir William Christopher, K.C.B., M.V.O. 6409
Commanders:
Creedy, Herbert James, Esq., C.B., M.V.O. 5462
Brand, Commodore the Hon. Hubert George, M.V.O. ... 6409

Royal Victorian Order (cont.):
Commanders (cont.):
Cruise, Richard Robert, F.R.C.S. (Eng.) 5462
Harris, Charles Alexander, C.B., C.M.G., M.V.O. ... 5462
Hawksley, Commodore James Rose Price, C.B. 6409
Lucas, Francis Herman, C.B. 5462
Power, Rear-Admiral Laurence Eliot, C.B., M.V.O. ... 6180
Verney, Harry Lloyd, M.V.O. 5462
Members of the Fourth Class:
Bacon, Edward Denny ... 5462
Burgoyne, Capt. Sydney Thomas 6180
Forrest, Arthur James ... 5462
Irvine, Capt. Charles Alexander Lindsay ... 5462
Paulet, Maj. Charles Standish 5462
Stavers, Capt. John 6180
Russia. Orders. (See under "Foreign Orders.")
Rutlandshire, Appeal Tribunal under Military Service Act ... 6410

S

St. Christopher and Nevis, Presidency of:
Executive Council, Official Member:
Fretz, William Henry ... 5515
Legislative Council, Official Members:
Fretz, William Henry ... 4499
Greaves, Charles Cocksage 4499
Jones, Edward Rutter ... 4499
Meggs, Edgar Ethelred ... 4499
Semper, Dudley Henry ... 4499
Wigley, Wilfred Murray ... 4499
Unofficial Members:
Conacher, Walter 4499
Marshall, Burchell 4499
Mills, Paithfield 4499
Parmenter, Robert Bernard 4499
Reid, Alexander Moir ... 4499
Shelford, Edward Jefferson... 4499
St. John of Jerusalem in England, Grand Priory of the Order of the Hospital of:
Knights of Justice:
Wales, H.R.H. Prince of, K.G., M.C. 5514
Knights of Grace:
Bartholomew, Charles William 6285
Begbie, Lt.-Col. Frank Warburton, M.R.C.S., L.R.C.P. 4215
de Grey, John Arthur Stamford 4215
Needham, George William ... 6285
Worthington, Major Sir Edward Scott, C.M.G., M.V.O., M.D. ... 4215
Hon. Knights of Grace:
Czarnanski, H. E. Anatole ... 4215
Hauser, Col. Carl 6285
Ignatieff, H. E. Boris ... 4215
Illyine, H. E. Alexis ... 4215
Ladies of Grace:
Clipperton, Ella Elizabeth, Mrs. 5357
Fox-Symons, Maude, Mrs. ... 6285
Henderson, Vesta Viola, Mrs. 4215
Hope, Mary, Lady St. John 5357
Malmesbury, The Countess of 6285
Maude, Mrs. Fox-Symons ... 6285
May, Helena Augusta Victoria, Lady 4215
Stevens, Edith, Mrs. ... 4215
Warren, Sarah Trumbull, Mrs. 4215

Figure 24 A *London Gazette* index entry, RRC 2nd Quarter, 1917 (ZJ 1/643)

covering January and February, the June edition also covering April and May, the September edition covering announcements also made in July and August, and the December edition taking in October and November. The arrangement of each index is similar: in alphabetical order by the name of the award and then in alphabetical order by name of recipient. Alongside each name is a page number of a *London Gazette* published with the quarter of the year the index covers. Make a note of the page number, the number of the index (i.e. which quarter it covers) and the year, and take the information to the ZJ 1 catalogue.

During the First World War period, each month of the *London Gazette* had a different number of pages, many running into the thousands. The first page of the first *London Gazette* in January of any year is always page 1. The last page of the last *London Gazette* of December in the same year may be over page 12,000. By matching the page number of the entry to the relevant *Gazette*, already knowing that it can have only come from one of three months, you should find the relevant entry quite easily.

There are a number of indexes and finding aids that can help you to find the award you seek and they are listed under the relevant awards.

On the card indexes of the DCM, MM and MSM, the date when the award was announced in the *London Gazette* is sometimes given as a number. These numbers and the corresponding dates are listed below:

Gazette No.	Date(s)
59	11 February or 13 March 1919
60	18 or 24 or 30 January or 22 February 1919
61	29 March 1919
62	14 May 1919
63	17 June 1919
64	3 July 1919
65	23 July 1919
66	20 August 1919
67	20 August 1919
68	22 September 1919
69	16 October 1919
Peace Gazette	3 June 1919

10.3 The Victoria Cross

The Victoria Cross (VC) is the supreme award for gallantry in face of the enemy and as such was instituted in 1856. Some 633 Victoria Crosses were awarded during the First World War, this figure including two bars for second awards to Arthur Martin-Leake and Noel Chavasse. All awards of the VC are announced in the *London Gazette* and are accompanied by citations.

Recommendations for the award of the VC were submitted on an Army Form W 3121 and had to be accompanied by at least three independent eyewitness statements. Once the recommendation paperwork had been passed up the chain of command, the final submission had to be passed to the Secretary of State for War and finally the King. The only complete submission that has survived (the remainder being destroyed in the Arnside Street fire on 8 September 1940) is that for Pte H. Christian, 2nd Battalion, King's Own Royal Lancaster Regiment, which can be found in WO 32/21402.

The register of the VC can be found in WO 98. This register contains, in *Gazette* date order, the citations and in many cases the date of death of all winners of the VC from the First World War. WO 98/5 contains a list of all VCs by division and unit. WO 98/6 is an alphabetical list of Victoria Crosses awarded from 1914 to 1920. The register for 1900–1944 is in WO 98/8.

10.4 The Distinguished Service Order

The Distinguished Service Order (DSO) was instituted in 1886 as a reward for meritorious or distinguished service. The award was initially for those officers not eligible for the CB (Companion of the Most Honourable Order of the Bath) but during the First World War the award was bestowed upon officers from the rank of 2nd Lieutenant to brigadier general. Once the Military Cross was instituted in 1914 (see section **10.5**), it was unusual for officers below lieutenant and even captain to be awarded the DSO.

Announcement of awards of the DSO can be found in the *London Gazette* (see section **10.2**). Awards announced as part of the New Year or Birthday Honours lists were primarily for meritorious service and not for gallantry in action, and as such these awards are not accompanied by a citation.

The 'Register of the DSO' can be found in WO 390 and is arranged by the date when the award was announced in the *London Gazette*. The entries in WO 390 provide the citation, the date when the award was presented to the recipient or when it was sent by post, and in some cases the date when the recipient died (even after the war). WO 390 is available on microfilm.

The DSO and MC Gazette Book in WO 389 contains advance copies of the *London Gazette* which were given to the War Office just prior to publication. These advance copies are arranged in chronological order and then by DSO and MC, and are then annotated in most cases with the place and date of the deed for which the award was being granted. The date and place can be used with information found in the war diaries in WO 95 (see section **7.3**).

The DSO and MC Gazette Books can be found in WO 389/1–8 and are available on microfilm.

Apart from using the *London Gazette* to find out when an award was gazetted, it is possible to find the date when the award was announced, and in some cases other biographical data, by consulting *The Distinguished Service Order* by General Sir O'Moore Creagh and Miss E. M. Humphris (1988), a copy of which is available in the PRO Library.

10.5 The Military Cross

The Military Cross (MC) was instituted in late 1914 as a reward for gallantry or meritorious service performed by officers of the rank of captain and below, and warrant officers. As with other decorations for gallantry or meritorious service, all awards of the Military Cross are announced in the *London Gazette* (see section **10.2**).

Although information regarding the MC can be found in the *London Gazette* (which can be time consuming), there is a name index together with annotated copies of the *London Gazette* on microfilm in the record series WO 389. WO 389/1–8, called the Gazette Books, are copies of the *London Gazette* which were kept by the War Office and then in many cases annotated with the date and place of the action for which the MC was awarded. WO 389/9–24 is the name index, which will provide name, rank and unit of the MC recipient and the date when the award was announced in the *London Gazette*. By applying the *Gazette* date to WO 389/1–8 you should be able to find the citation for the award.

MCs announced as part of the New Year or Birthday Honours lists were for meritorious service rather than gallantry in action and as such are not accompanied by a citation.

10.6 The Distinguished Conduct Medal

The Distinguished Conduct Medal (DCM) was instituted in 1854 as an award for all other ranks for distinguished service in the field. As with other awards, all awards of the DCM, apart from those to foreign nationals, are announced in the *London Gazette*. Most announcements are accompanied by a citation, but some awards announced in the New Year or Birthday Honours lists have no citations.

The DCM Gazette Books are in WO 391. A nominal card index of DCM recipients giving name, rank, number, unit and the date when the award was announced in the *London Gazette* is available in the Microfilm Reading Room.

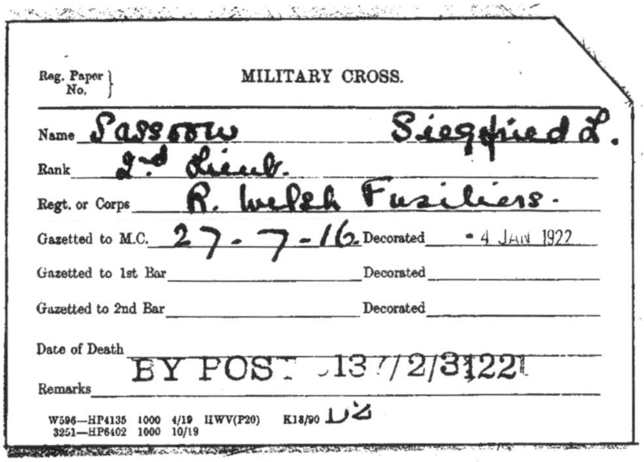

MILITARY CROSS.

Reg. Paper No.

Name Sassoon Siegfried L.

Rank 2nd Lieut.

Regt. or Corps R. Welsh Fusiliers.

Gazetted to M.C. 27-7-16 Decorated 4 JAN 1922

Gazetted to 1st Bar Decorated

Gazetted to 2nd Bar Decorated

Date of Death

Remarks BY POST 137/2/31221

W596—HP4135 1000 4/19 HWV(P20) K18/90 D2
3251—HP6402 1000 10/19

Figure 25 The Military Cross Index Card for Siegfried Sassoon's award (WO 389/21)

A published roll of the DCM can be found in *Recipients of the Distinguished Conduct Medal 1914–1920*, by R. W. Walker (1980). Once again this book provides the same data as the card index. The book is available in the PRO Library.

10.7 The Military Medal

The Military Medal (MM) was instituted in March 1916 and apart from two very early awards, the first awards were announced in the *London Gazette* on 3 June 1916. The MM was created as an award for warrant officers, NCOs and men. The award was also available to women.

A nominal index of MM winners giving name, rank, number, units and the *London Gazette* date, is available in the Microfilm Reading Room.

10.8 The Meritorious Service Medal

Originally conceived as an award for long and meritorious service for other ranks, the recipient also being awarded an annuity, the warrant of the Meritorious Service Medal (MSM) was altered during the First World War, due to the need for an award for service not in face of the enemy. From 1916 the MSM was awarded for meritorious service or gallantry not in face of the enemy but without an annuity. All awards of these non-annuity or what became known as immediate MSMs were announced in the *London Gazette*.

Cross.

35.

Lond. Gaz 27th July 1916.

five of his men and bringing his guns into action in a captured enemy position. He was under heavy shell fire the whole time. Later he did fine work, clearing the position. *Mametz. 1.7.16.*

• Temp. 2nd Lt. Arthur John Riley, 8th Bn., York. and Lanc. R. — 0137/2706.

For conspicuous gallantry and determination. When his patrol was attacked by a much stronger enemy bombing party, and he himself and all his patrol were wounded, he kept up the fight till the enemy was dispersed. He then returned with some of his wounded, and finally, in spite of his own wounds, went out again to bring in the remainder. He has repeatedly done fine work on patrol. *Aveluy. 17/18 June 1916.*

• Temp. 2nd Lt. Edward Lawrence Riley, 22nd Bn., Manch. R. — 0137/2745.

For conspicuous gallantry. When all the officers near him had become casualties he rallied the men and successfully organised a fresh advance. *Mametz. 1-5 July 1916.*

• 2nd Lt. Robert Blackwood Ritchie, 1st Bn., Sco. Rif. — 0137/2706.

For conspicuous gallantry during a raid on the enemy's trenches. He commanded an assaulting platoon, and personally accounted for two of the enemy and captured a third. The success of the raid was mainly due to his coolness and initiative. He has previously done fine work. *Cuinchy 4/5 June 1916.*

• Temp. 2nd Lt. Arthur Rought, 207th Fd. Co., R.E. — 0137/2743.

For conspicuous gallantry. He took command of a raiding party when the officer in charge had become a casualty, destroyed the enemy's wire and skilfully withdrew under heavy shell fire with only one man slightly wounded. *Heath Redan - near Albert 29/30 June 1916.*

• 2nd Lt. Sydney John Cenlivres Russell, Border R., Spec. Res. (attd. 2nd Bn.). — 0137/2745.

For conspicuous determination and initiative. He organised a machine-gun party and attacked and drove off an enemy machine gun which was holding up the advance. *N. of Mametz. 1.7.16.*

• 2nd Lt. Charles Michael Joseph Ryan, R. Muns. Fus., Spec. Res. (attd. 2nd Bn.). — 0137/2724.

For conspicuous gallantry during a raid on the enemy's lines. He attacked a bombing post, shot the defenders with his revolver, and directed the withdrawal after another officer had become a casualty. He set a fine example of personal bravery. *Calonne 25.6.16.*

• 2nd Lt. (temp. Lt.) Algernon Frederick Roland Dudley Ryder, "C" Bty., 5th Lond. Bde., R.F.A., T.F. (attd. C/235th Bty.). — 0137/2671.

For gallantry and devotion to duty. After two gun pits had been hit, most of the detachments knocked out, and the ammunition pit set on fire, Lt. Ryder put out the fire, got his guns into action again, and, though wounded, refused to leave the guns till ordered by his Battery Commander to do so. *Ablain. 21.5.16.*

• Temp. 2nd Lt. Charles Sainsbury, 1st Bn., Wilts. R. — 0137/2664.

For conspicuous gallantry and coolness. On two occasions he succeeded, by skilful leading, in occupying under heavy fire the

near lip of enemy crater immediately the hostile mine had been exploded. *E. of Mont St. Eloy. 3rd & 8th May 1916.*

• 2nd Lt. Siegfried Lorraine Sassoon, 3rd (attd. 1st) Bn., R. W. Fus. — 0137/2706.

For conspicuous gallantry during a raid on the enemy's trenches. He remained for 1½ hours under rifle and bomb fire collecting and bringing in our wounded. Owing to his courage and determination all the killed and wounded were brought in. *Fricourt 25/26 May 1916.*

• 2nd Lt. Thomas Scott, 4th (attd. 1st) Bn., Sco. Rif. — 0137/2719.

For conspicuous gallantry. After the explosion of a mine he went out in daylight and endeavoured to reach an officer and man who were lying half buried below the lip of the crater. It was chiefly due to his efforts that the two were rescued at night. *Cuinchy - 22.6.16.*

• 2nd Lt. Humphrey Basil Secretan, R.W. Surr. R., Spec. Res. (attd. 2nd Bn.). — 0137/2745.

For conspicuous gallantry. When all the officers of his company had become casualties he took command and did fine work capturing a position. *Mametz. 1-5 July 1916.*

• Temp. 2nd Lt. John Stanley Horsfall Shafto, 8th (S.) Bn., E. Kent R. — 0137/2664.

For gallantry in attempting by daylight, under fire, to rescue a man who had been blown out of his trench. He went over the parapet, returned for assistance, and remained with the man till he died. *Ploegsteert. 26.5.16.*

• 2nd Lt. (temp. Lt.) Cecil Moorhouse Slack, 1/4th Bn., E. York. R., T.F. — 0137/2724.

For conspicuous gallantry when leading a raiding party against the enemy trenches. He entered their trench alone, accounted for two of the enemy, and withdrew safely after fifteen minutes. *N. Wytschaete 26/27 June 1916.*

• Temp. 2nd Lt. Douglas George Smith, 6th Bn., Shrops. L.I. — 0137/2712.

For conspicuous gallantry on patrol. He went right up to the enemy's parapet, and, though wounded, remained out for two hours to verify what he had heard. He has shown great coolness and bravery on many occasions. *E. of Ypres. 18/19 June 1916.*

• 2nd Lt. (temp. Capt.) Joseph Snape, 1st Bn., S. Staff. R. — 0137/2745.

For conspicuous gallantry and good leadership during a successful assault on an enemy position. *Mametz. 1.7.16.*

• 2nd Lt. William Augustine Spain, 5th Bn., Essex R., T.F. (attd. 20th Mach. Gun Co.). — 0137/2743.

For conspicuous gallantry before and during the assault on an enemy position. He took his guns to the front line after the assault and inflicted heavy loss on the enemy, while his gun teams made many prisoners. He set a fine example to his men. *Mametz. 1.7.16.*

• 2nd Lt. Allan Spowers, 3rd Bn. (attd. 6th Bn.), E. Lan. R. — 0137/2746.

For conspicuous gallantry in leading a night attack on the enemy's position, although twice wounded. *Umm-el-Hannah - 5.4.16.* — MESOPOTAMIA. 0137/2854.

• Temp. 2nd Lt. Harold Nevill Stokoe, 9th (S.) Bn., N. Lan. R. — 0137/2671.

This officer was put in command of an

Figure 26 The citation for Sassoon's Military Cross (WO 389/2)

There is a card index in the Microfilm Reading Room listing awards of the MSM. The card index provides name, rank, number, regiment or corps, which operational theatre the award was won in, and the date when the award was announced in the *London Gazette*. The card index is arranged in alphabetical order.

A complete list of all the immediate MSMs awarded between 1916 and 1928 when the award was replaced by the British Empire Medal (BEM) can be found in *Meritorious Service Medal. The Immediate Awards 1916–1928* by Ian McInnes (1988), a copy of which is available in the PRO Library.

10.9 Mentioned in Despatches

The award of a Mentioned in Despatches (MiD) was the lowest form of recognition for service performed during the war which was announced in the *London Gazette*. Originally only an award which was recorded on paper (on the record of service), towards the end of the war there was a call for some form of visible mark to show that an individual had been given an MiD. After much discussion, the government decided to allow an oakleaf emblem to be worn on the ribbon of the Victory Medal. Only one oakleaf emblem could be worn, however many times an individual was Mentioned in Despatches. Along with the oakleaf, each time an individual was mentioned, he would receive a certification bearing his full service details, the date and author of the despatch and the date it was announced in the *London Gazette*.

An incomplete index of those who were Mentioned in Despatches, providing service details and the *Gazette* date, is available in the Microfilm Reading Room.

10.10 The Royal Red Cross

Instituted in 1883 as a reward for nurses, the Royal Red Cross (RRC) was further expanded in 1915 by the addition of a second class award, the Associate of the Royal Red Cross (ARRC). Any nurses awarded an ARRC could be promoted within the award and awarded an RRC. In 1917 a bar was authorized for the RRC only. Any nurse who was already holding an ARRC and who was awarded the award again, was given an RRC.

All awards are announced in the *London Gazette*. The register of the Royal Red Cross (both classes) is in WO 145.

An RRC, together with the other awards given to Sister F. M. Rice, can be seen on the frontispiece to this book.

SUPPLEMENT to the LONDON GAZETTE, 4 JUNE, 1917.   5487

Lt. Mervyn Roy Walker, N.Z. Force.
Capt. Herbert Henry Whyte, N.Z. Fld. Arty.
2nd Lt. Edward Gordon Williams, Mtd. Rifles.
Capt. Richard William Wrightson, N.Z. Force.

SOUTH AFRICAN FORCES.

Capt. Fritz Baumann Adler, S.A. Fld. Arty.
Capt. Rudolph John Bell, S.A.S.C.
Capt. Edgar Frederick Bradstock.
Capt. Ferdinand Lindley Augustus Buchanan, S.A. Inf.
2nd Lt. Frederick William Severine Burton, S.A. Inf.
Lt. Dennis St. John Clowes, S.A. Fld. Arty.
Capt. William Charles Cock, S.A. Forces.
T./Capt. Stephanus Nicolaus Cronje, 1st S.A.R.
T./Capt. Joseph Atkinson Dingwall, R.E.
Capt. Dudley Fenn, S.A.S.C.
T./Lt. David Joshua Hamer.
Capt. Edgar Henry Malachi Hardiman, S.A. Inf.
Capt. Leonard Norman Hay, S.A. Inf.
Capt. Andrew George Hendri, B.S.A. Police.
Capt. Frederick Ernest Jackson, S.A. Sig. Coy.
Capt. Stanley Conway John, S.A. Rifles.
Lt. (T./Capt.) Hugh Marston Ladell, S.A. S.C., Eng. Serv.
Capt. Robert Patrick McNeill, S.A.M.C.
2nd Lt. Neville William Methven, S.A. Sharpshooters.
Capt. George James Moore, S.A. Eng. Troop.
Lt. (now T./Maj.) Montague Headland Pike, S.A.M.R.
T./Capt. George Herbert Bonsier Raymond. S.A. Forces.
Capt. Adrian Murray Robertson, S.A.S.C.
Lt. (T./Capt.) James Robertson, S.A. Inf.
Capt. Charles Duncan Cogwell Smuts, S.A.S.C.
T./Capt. Leslie Francis Sprenger, S.A. Inf.
Capt. Francis Trant Stevens, B.S.A. Police.
Lt. Harold Swifte, S.A. Mtd. Rif.
Capt. Reginald Tomlinson, S.A. Inf.
Capt. Daniel Peter Wessel Van Zyl, S.A. Eng. Troops.
Capt. (now T./Maj.) Chapl. William Hall Watson, S A Chapl. Dept.
Capt. Percival Frederick Foylan White, S.A. Inf.
Lt. Thomas H. Wilson, S.A. Engrs.

His Majesty the KING has been graciously pleased to award the Royal Red Cross Decoration to the undermentioned Ladies, in recognition of their valuable services with the Armies in the Field :—

ROYAL RED CROSS, 1st CLASS.

Miss Gertrude Mary Allen, A/Matron, Q.A.I.M.N.S.
Miss Hilda Davidge, Assistant Matron, T.F.N.S.
Miss Eva Cicely Fox, A.R.R.C., A/Matron, Q.A.I.M.N.S.
Miss Anne McInnis Forrest, Nursing Sister, Canadian A.M.C.
Miss Elizabeth Clement Humphreys, Matron, Q.A.I.M.N.S.

Miss Frances Rosa Holmes, A/Matron, Q.A.I.M.N.S.
Miss Mollie Jones, Sister (acting Matron), T.F.N.S.
Miss Edith Mary Lyde, A.R.R.C., A/Matron, Q.A.I.M.N.S.
Miss Rose Emmeline Lumsden, Sister (acting Matron), Q.A.I.M.N.S.R.
Miss Ethel Jane Minns, A.R.R.C., A/Matron, Q.A.I.M.N.S.
Miss Annie Cecilia Mowat, A.R.R.C., A/Matron, Q.A.I.M.N.S.
Miss Maude Leslie Martin, Matron, T.F.N.S.
Miss Jean Matheson, Nursing Sister (acting Asst. Matron), Canadian A.N.S.
Miss Laura Niven, Matron, S.A.M.N.S., Hospl. Ship.
Miss Patricia A. O'Curran, Sister (acting Matron), Q.A.I.M.N.S.R.
Mrs. Edith Helen Phillips, A.R.R.C., Nursing Service.
Miss Frances Maude Rice, A.R.R.C., Sister, T.F.N.S.
Miss Jessie Smales, Sister (act. Asst. Matron), T.F.N.S.
Miss Marion Smith, A.R.R.C., A/Matron, Q.A.I.M.N.S.
Miss Ada Taylor, Assistant Matron, T.F.N.S.
Miss Lorna Beatrice Wood, Montaza Palace Hospl.

ROYAL RED CROSS, 2nd CLASS.

Miss Mary Ashlin-Thomas, Matron, B.R.C.S.
Miss Mary Macdonald Aitkin, Acting Sister, Q.A.I.M.N.S.R.
Miss Gertrude Jean Arthur, Staff Nurse, T.F.N.S.
Miss Frances Mary Louisa Allen, Sister, T.F.N.S.
Miss Helen Aukett, Nursing Service.
Miss Elsie Blackburn, Staff Nurse, T.F.N.S.
Miss Jennie Wilhelmina Blyth, A/Sister, Civil Hospl. Reserve (Glasgow Royal).
Miss Louise Brock, Nursing Sister, Canadian A.N.S.
Miss Jean Binnie Buckham, Sister, Q.A.I.M.N.S.R., Australia.
Miss Edith Barker, Sister, S.A.M.N.S.
Miss Ellen Elizabeth Baldrey, Sister, Q.A.I.M.N.S.R.
Miss Edith Frances Coombe, Sister, B.R.C.S.
Miss Gertrude Emily Custance, A/Sister, Q.A.I.M.N.S.R.
Miss Mary Coupar, Sister, T.F.N.S.
Miss Jean Elizabeth Carter, Staff Nurse, Q.A.I.M.N.S.R., 15th British Stat. Hospl.
Miss Effie Sloan Clark, Sister, T.F.N.S.
Miss Annie Eleanor Casserley, Acting Sister, Civil Hospital Reserve (Liverpool Southern).
Miss Annie Harriet Esden, A/Matron, Q.A.I.M.N.S.
Miss Winifred Ayre Evers, Acting Sister, Civil Hospl. Reserve (Edinburgh Royal Infirmary).
Miss Mary Amilia Early, Staff Nurse, N.Z.A.N.S.
Miss Mary Gladys Foley, A/Sister, Q.A.I.M.N.S.
Miss Alice Louisa Florence FitzGerald, Acting Sister, Q.A.I.M.N.S.R.
Miss Kathleen Fisher, V.A.D.
Miss Margaret Grieg, A/Sister, Civil Hospl. Reserve (Gt. Northern Central).
Miss Harriet Graham, Nursing Sister, Canadian A.M.C.
Miss Sybil Senior Gardiner, Sister, Q.A.I.M.N.S.R.

Figure 27 A *London Gazette* award anouncement (ZJ 1/645)

10.11 The Order of British India

Originally instituted in 1839, the OBI was a reward for meritorious service and was awarded in two classes to Indian commissioned officers. As with other awards the OBI was announced in the *London Gazette*.

10.12 The Indian Order of Merit

The Indian Order of Merit (IOM) was instituted by the Honourable East India Company in 1837. During the First World War period the award was available in two classes and was awarded to native Indian soldiers. Awards of the IOM were announced in the *London Gazette*.

10.13 The Indian Distinguished Service Medal

Instituted in 1907 as an award for Indian commissioned officers, non-commissioned officers and other ranks of the Indian Army, awards of the IDSM were announced in the *London Gazette*. A bar for subsequent awards was authorized in 1917 and the award was extended to those non-combatants serving in the field.

10.14 Orders of Chivalry

The award of any order of chivalry was announced in the *London Gazette*. The most common awards made prior to 1917 were to the Most Honourable Order of the Bath and the Most Distinguished Order of Saint Michael and Saint George. These awards were only open to officers. The Most Excellent Order of the British Empire which was instituted in 1917 was open to warrant officers and above. *Burke's Handbook of the Order of the British Empire* of 1921 lists all appointments to the Order between 1917 and late 1920. A copy of this book is available in the PRO Library.

10.15 Records of the India Office

Although all awards for gallantry and meritorious service to members of the British and Indian Armies are announced in the *London Gazette*, one file, in the British Library, is worth consulting above all others. L/MIL/17/5/2416 contains a list of awards granted to Indian Officers (Native), NCOs and men and followers of the Indian Army and Imperial Service Troops (Indian State Forces) in all theatres during the First World War. Broken down by award from the VC down, this book provides full service details, where the award was earned and any salient remarks. The work also includes foreign awards, promotions and gratuities.

10.16 Recommendations for awards

Recommendations for awards were submitted on an Army Form W 3121, the vast majority of which were destroyed in the fire at the War Office records repository in Arnside Street in London on 8 September 1940. Some recommendations for awards may be found amongst the files concerning operations in East Africa. One file concerning recommendations for awards to members of the WAAC for the period December 1918 to December 1919 can be found in WO 165/65.

10.17 Citations

A citation is the brief description of the deed for which an award was granted, and it usually accompanies the announcement of the award when published in the *London Gazette*. In many cases the citation was published later than the announcement. In most cases it is possible to find the publication of the citation by consulting the index of the *London Gazette*. See section **10.2** for further information.

No citations were published for awards announced in the New Year and Birthday Honours lists. Also, apart from those for a number of Military Medals awarded to nurses, no citations were published for the majority of MMs announced between 1916 and 1919.

10.18 Foreign awards

Many men and women of the British Army were given awards by our allies. Many awards given to personnel of the British Army were announced in the *London Gazette*. However, a significant number of awards, especially those given to other ranks were not announced in the *London Gazette*.

Records concerning foreign awards given to Britons can be found in WO 388, which lists by bestowing country and *London Gazette* date, the names of those individuals who received such awards as the Croix de Guerre and Legion of Honour. The records in WO 388 also list a number of awards which were not announced in the *London Gazette*, especially those given in the early months of the war.

WO 388 is available on microfilm.

11 | Courts martial

11.1 Introduction

Thousands of men were tried by court martial for offences committed during the First World War. Depending upon the offence committed, the type of court martial where the accused was tried dictates whether any records survive concerning the case.

Apart from the registers of courts martial in WO 213, which lists all those tried by court martial, the only other major source are the proceedings of courts martial which concern primarily those where the accused was executed.

Military Information Leaflet 22, 'Army: Courts Martial, 17th–20th Centuries' can provide some basic information.

11.2 Courts martial proceedings WO 71

The records preserved in the record series WO 71 consist of trial proceedings of those courts martial held to try the most serious military crimes. The majority of the files are for men executed for murder, desertion and other offences which carried the death penalty. Arranged in chronological order by date of trial, it is possible to search the on-line catalogue by name of the accused.

An example of a WO 71 record can be seen in **Fig 28**. The subject of this example, Private William Nelson 14 DLI, is pictured on the cover of *Death Sentences* by Gerard Oram.

11.3 Registers of courts martial

Registers of Field General Courts Martial, containing the names of the accused, his rank, regiment or corps, place of trial, charge and sentence, can be found in WO 213/ 2–26. Registers of District Courts Martial containing similar information but for lesser offences can be found in WO 86/62–65. Registers of General Courts Martial which took place abroad are in WO 90/6–8.

If an individual was tried by court martial, the date and place where the trial took

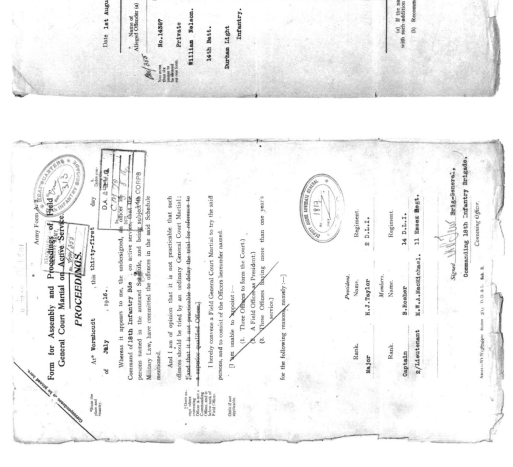

Figure 28 A typical example of a Court Martial Proceedings Paper (WO 71/488)

place, together with the charge(s) and if found guilty, the sentence, should be annotated on the individual's AF B103 Casualty Form – Active Service. Details concerning courts martial may also be found on the Regimental, Company or Field Conduct Sheet, Army Form B 121 or B 122.

An example of a WO 213 register can be seen in **Fig 29**.

11.4 Other courts martial records

The only other significant records concerning courts martial are the records kept in WO 93. Amongst these records are nominal rolls for Australians tried by court martial in WO 93/42, and Canadians tried by court martial in WO 93/43–45.

11.5 Published sources

There are a number of very important books concerning courts martial, many of which provide information not only about the cases but also about the accused.

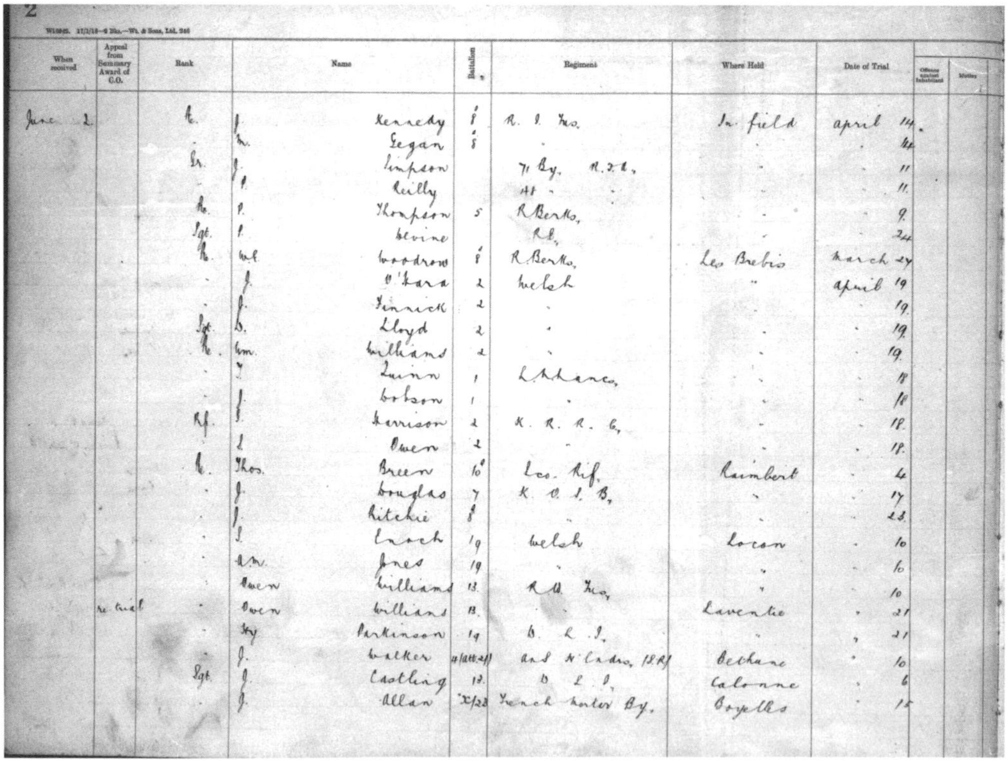

When received	Appeal from Summary Award of C.O.	Rank	Name	Battalion	Regiment	Where Held	Date of Trial	Offence against Inhabitant	Mutiny
June 2.		Pte.	J. Kennedy	8	R. I. Fus.	In field	April 14		
		·	M. Gegan	8	·	·	· 14		
		Gr.	J. Simpson		71 By. R.F.A.	·	· 11		
		·	P. Reilly		41 · ·	·	· 11		
		Pte.	P. Thompson	5	R. Berks.	·	· 9		
		Sgt.	P. Levine		R.E.	·	· 24		
		Pte.	Wm. Woodrow	8	R. Berks.	Les Brebis	March 27		
		·	J. O'Hara	2	Welsh	"	April 19		
		·	J. Fenwick	2	·	·	· 19		
		Sgt.	D. Lloyd	2	·	·	· 19		
		Pte.	Wm. Williams	2	·	·	· 19		
		·	T. Quinn	1	L. N. Lancs.	·	· 18		
		·	J. Dobson	1	·	·	· 18		
		Rfn.	J. Harrison	2	K. R. R. C.	·	· 18		
		·	J. Owen	2	·	·	· 18		
		Pte.	Thos. Breen	10	Lco. Rif.	Raimbert	· 4		
		·	J. Douglas	7	K. O. S. B.	·	· 17		
		·	J. Ritchie	8	·	·	· 23		
		·	S. Enoch	19	Welsh	Locon	· 10		
		·	A.M. Jones	19	·	·	· 10		
		·	Owen Williams	13.	R. W. Fus.	·	· 10		
	re-trial	·	Owen Williams	13.	·	Laventie	· 21		
		·	Hy Parkinson	19	D. L. I.	·	· 21		
		·	J. Walker	4/(att. 21)	and N. Cadre, 18 R.I.	Bethune	· 10		
		Sgt.	J. Castling	13.	D. L. I.	Calonne	· 6		
		·	J. Allan	X/23	Trench Mortar By.	Boyelles	· 15		

Figure 29 A Court Martial Register (WO 213/9)

Copies of all the following can be found in the PRO Library.

Death Sentences Passed by Military Courts of the British Army 1914–1920 by Gerard Oram (1998). This book, arranged alphabetically, lists all those sentenced to death, even if the sentence was commuted, and provides rank, number, regiment and offence. This book also provides PRO document references.

British Army Mutineers 1914–1922 by Julian Putkowski (1999) lists by name all those tried for mutiny and provides service details, PRO document references and some contextual information about the mutinies.

Officers Court Martialled by the British Army 1913–1924 by Gerard Oram and Julian Putkowski (2001) lists some 6,000 officers tried by court martial and once again provides service information and PRO document references.

The definitive work on those soldiers executed during the First World War is *Shot at Dawn*, by Julian Putkowski and Julian Sykes (1998). This book not only provides brief information about each case, but also information regarding those executed and numerous PRO document references can be found.

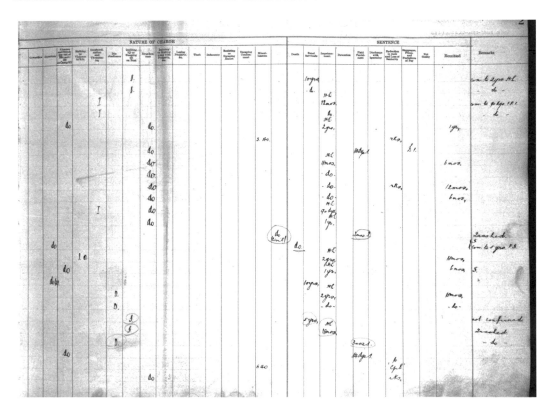

12 Prisoners of war

12.1 Introduction

During the First World War some 7,335 officers and 174,491 men were captured by the enemy, and most interestingly about half of this number fell into German hands between 21 March and 11 November 1918. Many other officers and men were captured in other operational theatres.

Although there are numerous records concerning prisoners of war, the majority being Foreign Office correspondence concerning prison camps and the care of the men being held in them, the most informative records concerning capture and life as a prisoner are those found in WO 161. In the case of officers who were captured, it is also possible to find their repatriation reports.

12.2 WO 161

A small selection of prisoner of war debrief records can be found in WO 161/95–101. These records were created by the Committee on the Treatment of British Prisoners of War and contain interviews and reports and are split into officers, WO 161/95–96, medical officers WO 161/97 and other ranks WO 161/98–100. The index to these papers is in WO 161/101. The index contains name, subject and place indexes. A copy of this index is held behind the staff desk in the Research Enquiries Room.

An example of one of these reports can be seen in **Fig 30**.

12.3 Repatriation reports

All those officers who were captured and who returned home after the war had to complete a report into the circumstances of their capture. The main purpose of these reports was to ascertain the conduct of the officer and to ensure that he had not surrendered in suspicious circumstances.

On the Medal Index Cards of many officers can be found the term 'Exonerated Officers List'. This was a list of officers who had been prisoners of war, and after their

INTERVIEW WITH CAPTAIN HORACE GRAY GILLILAND,
3RD LOYAL NORTH LANCASHIRE REGIMENT.

Convoy House, Donegal.

Immediately on the outbreak of war I applied for a commission, joined my unit and was posted to the 1st battalion. In December, 1914, we were in reserve at Hazebruck, when the Indians who were holding the position before La Bassée were driven out of their trenches, and we were brought up in a hurry to correct the position which had been created by their retirement.

The division to which I was attached was ordered to carry the three lines of trenches which had been taken, and Sir Douglas Haig himself was on the ground less than 300 yards from the enemy's trenches directing the operations. He told us that we must take and hold the trenches for 24 hours to give him a chance of digging in behind us. The whole division charged, the trenches were retaken and the front line occupied and, as well as we could do so, consolidated. We had no other tools than our entrenching tools. We had 150 rounds of ammunition, no bombs, no machine guns and practically no artillery to support us.

We held the trench until December 22nd, by which time our ammunition was exhausted and the Germans were lobbing bombs into the trench and doing great execution amongst our men. I found myself the only officer left, and had, in addition to my company about half a company of the Northamptons, whom I had found on our left and who were officerless.

On the 22nd December, between 3 and 4 p.m.—at La Bassée—the enemy came over and I was taken prisoner. I had been wounded at a much earlier period in the right ankle, and had a severe gunshot wound of the pleura [apparently perforation of pleura wall by ends of rib broken by fragment of shell, which did not, however, cause any important flesh wound—EXAMINER]. I had plugged the wound in my ankle with iodine. Whilst in the trench I had been hit in the side by a bit of shell which had broken three or four of my ribs. Before that I was able to hobble up and down the trench with the aid of a stick, but when the enemy reached our trenches I was practically "out," although, as it proved, I was still able to walk under compulsion, though such an effort gave me very great pain.

The enemy regiment which entered our trenches was, I believe, the 57th Bavarian—it was certainly a Bavarian regiment—and no sooner had they entered the trenches than they went to work systematically to bayonet such of our men as remained alive. Possibly because I was an officer I was spared, as also were three men in my immediate vicinity, all of whom were badly wounded. I saw the Germans do this terrible work and I also heard the screams of our wounded who were lying out behind the trench as they were slaughtered. I was taken before an officer, whose name I do not know, and was treated fairly civilly. He took away my papers and handed me and my three men to an escort. All four of us were badly wounded and could not by any stretch of imagination be described as walking cases, but we were compelled to walk first across No Man's Land and then through the enemy's communicating trenches towards La Bassée. Two of my men were walking before me. One was wounded in the head and was practically blinded. Another was shot through the stomach. The third man who followed me was also badly wounded in the body and constantly stopped from sheer pain, twice collapsing, being pricked on again by the sentry's bayonet. I could not offer him any help because it was as much as I could do to half crawl and half walk myself, but after he had collapsed twice I went back to him and said, "You must do your "best. You saw how they treated our wounded." He replied, "I can't go on, sir." I encouraged him by telling him it was not much farther to go and he made another effort. Presently he collapsed again and lay moaning on the ground. The sentry said something in German and then shortening his rifle he bayoneted the man on the ground and when I cursed him he threatened me. I do not recall

Capture. La Bassée, Dec. 22, 1914.

a (83)0410—298 11 50 6/17 E & S

Figure 30 An officer's report of his time as a prisoner of war (WO 161/96)

repatriation report had been considered and accepted by the committee set up to examine, were then permitted to be awarded their campaign medals. This list no longer exists.

An example of a repatriation report can be seen in **Fig 31**.

12.4 Other sources

A printed list of officers who became prisoners of war can be found in *List of Officers taken prisoner in the Various Theatres of War between August 1914 and November 1918*, compiled by the Military Agents Cox and Co. A copy of this book can be found in the PRO Library.

A number of lists of prisoners of war can be found amongst the ADM and AIR record series but they are not at all comprehensive. Correspondence concerning prisoners of war can be found in FO 383 Foreign Office: Prisoners of War and Aliens Department: General Correspondence from 1915–1919, which, whilst not containing full lists, is liberally scattered with names. This series is accessed by using the card index and registers in FO 566 and FO 662.

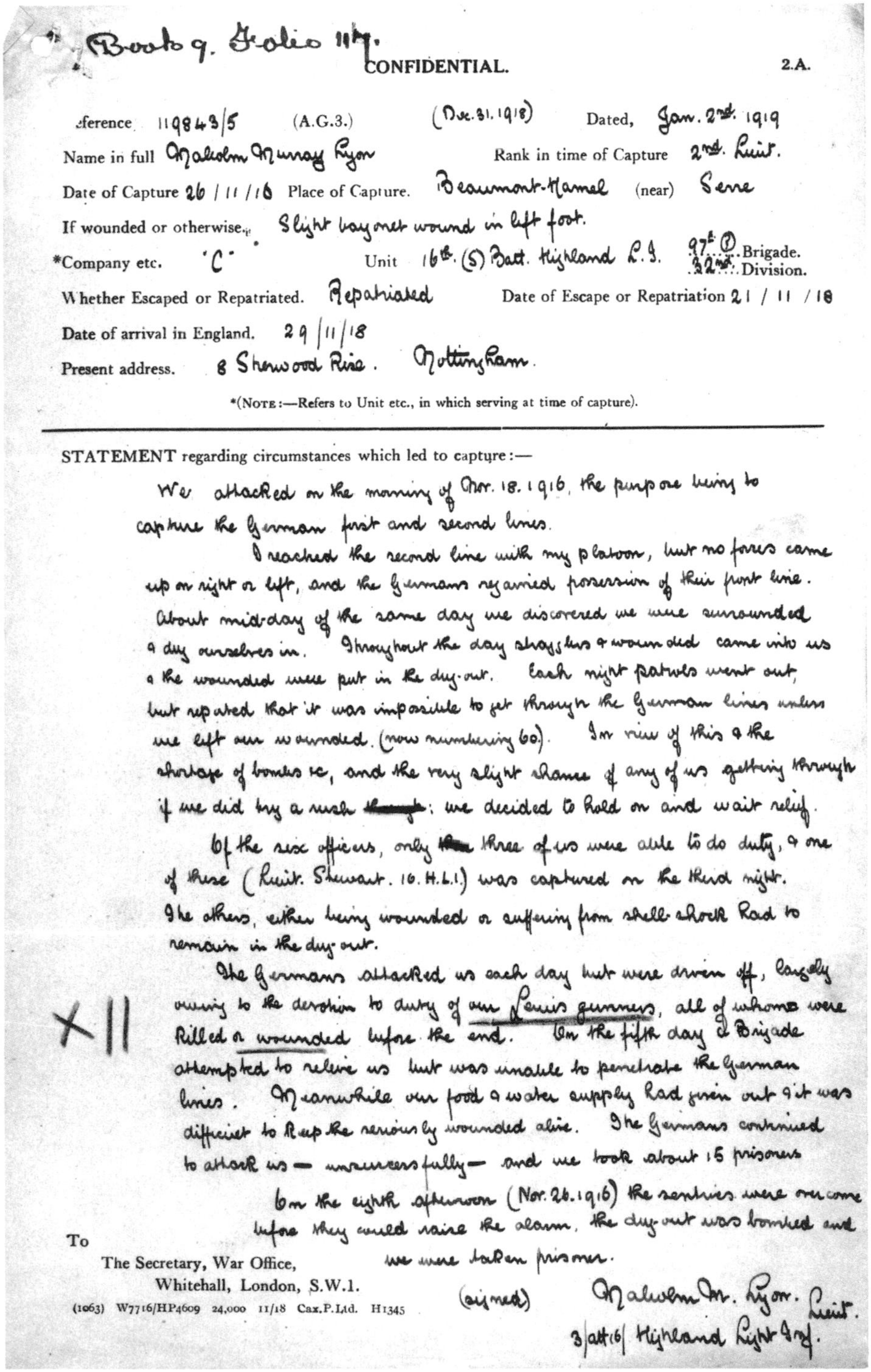

Book 9. Folio 114.

CONFIDENTIAL.

2.A.

Reference 11984 3/5   (A.G.3.)   (Dec. 31. 1918)   Dated, Jan. 2nd 1919

Name in full Malcolm Murray Lyon   Rank in time of Capture 2nd Lieut.

Date of Capture 26 / 11 /16 Place of Capture. Beaumont-Hamel (near) Serre

If wounded or otherwise. Slight bayonet wound in left foot.

*Company etc.   'C'   Unit 16th (S) Batt. Highland L.I. 97th ① Brigade. 32nd Division.

Whether Escaped or Repatriated. Repatriated   Date of Escape or Repatriation 21 / 11 / 18

Date of arrival in England. 29 /11/18

Present address. 8 Sherwood Rise. Nottingham.

*(NOTE:—Refers to Unit etc., in which serving at time of capture).

STATEMENT regarding circumstances which led to capture:—

We attacked on the morning of Nov. 18. 1916, the purpose being to capture the German first and second lines.

I reached the second line with my platoon, but no forces came up on right or left, and the Germans regained possession of their front line. About mid-day of the same day we discovered we were surrounded & dug ourselves in. Throughout the day stragglers & wounded came into us & the wounded were put in the dug-out. Each night patrols went out, but reported that it was impossible to get through the German lines unless we left our wounded (now numbering 60). In view of this & the shortage of bombs &c, and the very slight chance of any of us getting through if we did try a rush ———; we decided to hold on and wait relief.

Of the six officers, only three of us were able to do duty, & one of these (Lieut. Stewart. 16. H.L.I.) was captured on the third night. The others, either being wounded or suffering from shell shock had to remain in the dug-out.

The Germans attacked us each day but were driven off, largely owing to the devotion to duty of our Lewis gunners, all of whom were killed or wounded before the end. On the fifth day a Brigade attempted to relieve us but was unable to penetrate the German lines. Meanwhile our food & water supply had given out & it was difficult to keep the seriously wounded alive. The Germans continued to attack us — unsuccessfully — and we took about 15 prisoners.

On the eighth afternoon (Nov. 26.1916) the sentries were overcome before they could raise the alarm, the dug-out was bombed and we were taken prisoner.

(signed) Malcolm M. Lyon. Lieut.
3/att 16/ Highland Light Inf.

×||

To

The Secretary, War Office,
    Whitehall, London, S.W.1.

(1063) W7716/HP4609 24,000 11/18 Cax.P.Ltd. H1345

Figure 31 An example of an officer's Repatriation Report (WO 339/49656)

13 Casualties and war dead

13.1 Introduction

During the First World War the British Empire suffered over 2 million casualties and nearly 1 million men and women were killed. Specific records concerning the dead are very inconsistent in the information they provide. It is frequently the case that no records can be found. If no information is found in the unit war diary (see section **7.3**) then there are a number of other sources that can be consulted but they are not comprehensive. If papers exist for a soldier who lost his life during the war it is possible that an Army Form B 2090A Field Service Report of Death of a Soldier may be found in his records. This form provides full service details together with the date and place of death and the cause.

13.2 Hospital records

Hospital records held by the Public Record Office fall into four distinct types each of which is described below.

First, all medical units serving overseas had to complete a unit war diary. These diaries can be found in WO 95 and are more fully explained in section **7.3**. Although the diaries provide a day-to-day account of the events concerning the medical unit, in many cases they also list the names of those who died whilst in their care, giving unit details and in many cases the cause of death. An example of a casualty list from a unit war diary can be seen in **Fig 32**.

Secondly, the records held in MH 106 are a 2 per cent sample and represent the records used to compile an Official Medical History of the war (*History of the Great War based on Official Documents: Medical Services: Casualties and Medical Statistics of the Great War*). These records comprise three distinct groups: medical unit admission and discharge records; patient records; and records concerning certain types of wounds and diseases. There is a list of the medical unit records held in this record series at the beginning of the MH 106 catalogue. The medical units covered by these records include units that served at home and/or overseas.

Thirdly, the patient records are split into unit records and records organized by

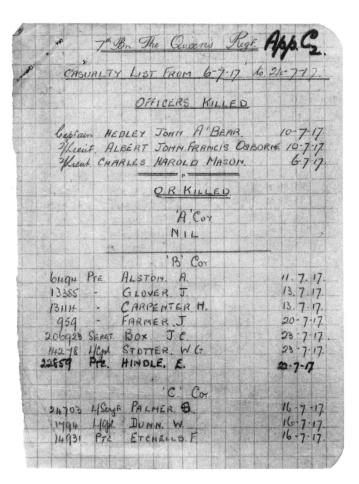

wound type. The units covered by MH 106 include the Royal Horse Artillery, a number of Hussar Regiments, the Grenadier Guards, Leicester Regiment and the Royal Flying Corps. These unit records are arranged in case sheet number. If you know that an individual from one of these units was wounded during the war, you may find some more medical records apart from those preserved with their record of service, in MH 106.

Amongst the records concerning diseases and wounds can be found files on patients suffering from gas poisoning, bayonet wounds and gun shot wounds in various parts of the body.

Fourthly, the admission and discharge books in MH 106 represent only a small number of medical units from home and overseas. Preserved amongst the collection in MH 106 is the admission register for Craiglockhart Hospital where Siegfried Sassoon and Wilfred Owen were both patients. An example of an admission register can be seen in **Fig 33**.

13.3 Disability pensions

The most significant collection of papers concerning disability pensions are the records in PIN 26. Information about these records can be found in section **2.9** for officers, section **3.5** for other ranks and section **4.4** for nurses.

Payment of disability pensions to officers made by the Paymaster General can be found in PMG 42.

13.4 War dead

There are two major secondary sources available in the PRO that can provide data about those men and women who died during the war, whether they were killed in action, died of wounds or disease, an accident or even natural causes. *Soldiers Died in the Great War* and *Officers Died in the Great War* list those who died during the war, and provide unit details, place and date of death and in many cases other unit details if they had served in another unit from that in which they died. Originally arranged by unit and then in alphabetical order, now that both of these works are available on CD ROM, it is possible to do a simple name search. *Soldiers* is also available on microfilm, and *Officers* in book form. Both of these sources only cover deaths between 4 August 1914 and 11 November 1918.

Weekly casualty returns of Indian Army Officers are held by the British Library under the reference L/MIL/14/139–140. An alphabetical list of Indian Army Officer casualties giving name, rank, unit, date and place of death and cause can be found in L/MIL/14/142.

The Commonwealth War Graves Commission (formerly the Imperial War Graves Commission) has a computerized database of all of those men and women who lost their lives during the two World Wars, and unlike *Soldiers* and *Officers Died*, the database covers those who died from after 11 November 1918, whose death could be attributed to war service. This database is available on the Internet at http://www.cwgc.org.uk. Access to the Commonwealth War Graves Commission website can be made at the PRO and printouts of individual entries can be obtained.

13.5 Deceased soldiers' effects

When a soldier died in service, in whatever circumstances, the Army would endeavour to ensure that his estate and certain personal effects were returned to the next of kin. The records concerning deceased soldiers' effects for the First World War are held by the National Army Museum and the information they contain includes, name, rank and number, unit, place of death (usually the operational theatre), date of death, financial value of estate and to whom it was passed. Unfortunately at the time of writing these records were not accessible.

In the case of officers who died during the war, details concerning their estates can usually be found in their records of service if they have survived. See **Chapter 2** for further details.

13.6 Widows' and dependants' pensions

Brief details concerning the pensions paid to a number of widows whose husbands died between 1914 and 1918 can be found in PIN 82.

PIN 82 consists of 183 separate pieces, each listing 50 servicemen. They provide very basic service data about the deceased, including unit data, date and place of death, and information about the widow and any children, including place of residence and the amount of pension they were granted. A list of names of those whose details can be found in PIN 82, can be found at the beginning of the PIN 82 catalogue.

A different collection of widows' pensions can be found in PIN 26/17179–19720. These files are arranged by name of the deceased.

A small collection of files of dependants' pensions can be found in PIN 26/19821–19853 and are arranged by name of dependant (usually children).

13.7 The memorial plaque and scroll

At the end of the war, the next of kin of all those men and women who had lost their lives during the war or whose death was attributed to war service up to seven years after the war had ended (11 November 1925), were given a memorial plaque and scroll bearing the full name of the deceased. The plaque is often called the 'Dead Man's Penny' or 'Death Plaque'. Examples of a plaque and scroll can be seen in **Fig 34** and **35**.

13.8 Other printed rolls

There are numerous published casualty rolls and other rolls of honour. Many casualty rolls can be found on the Internet.

Examples of rolls held by the PRO include the rolls of honour of the Midland Railway (RAIL 491/1259), the London, Brighton and South Coast Railway (RAIL 414/791) and the North Eastern Railway (RAIL 527/993).

ADMISSION AND DISCHARGE BOOK

_____ HOSPITAL

Index number of admissions. Transfers are not to be numbered consecutively with the admissions, but should be left un-numbered, or numbered in red ink as a separate series	Regiment, Battalion, Corps, or other unit	Squadron, Battery, or Company	Regtl. No.	Rank	Surname Christian Name	Completed years of		Completed months with Field Force	DISEASES (Wounds and injuries in action to be entered according to classification on fly leaf)
						Age	Service		
380ᵀ	Lancs Fus.			Lt.	Cronchley H.	21	2 10/12	9/12	Neurasthenia
381ᵀ	17 att. 2/1 London			2 Lt.	Bark K.	27	2 9/12	5/12	Neurasthenia
382ᵀ	7 Yorks			Lt.	Sherwood F.	32	14 yrs.	8/12	Neurasthenia
383ᵀ	7 Yorks			2 Lt.	Hartley F.E.	34	1 3/12	3/12	Neurasthenia
384ᵀ	R.E.			Cap.	Webb M.W.T.	28	9	2 2/12	Neurasthenia
385ᵀ	5ᵗʰ S.R.			2 Lt.	Clarkson D.D.	30	2 3/12	1 2/12	Neurasthenia
✓ 386ᵀ	H.A.C.			2 Lt.	Bosomworth W.F.	21	1 5/12	5/12	Neurasthenia
387ᵀ	R.F.C.			2 Lt.	Dudbridge M.	19	1 yr.	2/12	Neurasthenia
388ᵀ	10 att. 22 London Regt.			Lt.	Phillips R.W.	23	2 8/12	1/12	Neurasthenia
389ᵀ	21ˢᵗ Manchesters			2 Lt.	Whitworth J.C.	29	5 6/12	6/12	Neurasthenia
390ᵀ	R.F.a.			Lt.	Westwood a	36	1 yr.	4/12	Neurasthenia
391ᵀ	2ⁿᵈ Yorks			Lt.	Bell James	31	13 yrs	1 yr	Neurasthenia
392ᵀ	1ˢᵗ Dorsets			Major	Hope L.C.	44	20 7/12	1 11/12	Neurasthenia
393ᵀ	11ᵗʰ Lon. att. R.F.C. (16 Sqdn)			2 Lt.	Hale, H.R	24	2 9/12	1 3/12	Neurasthenia
394ᵀ	20ᵗʰ Manchesters			Capt.	Harford J.F.	49	2 5/12	1 3/12	Neurasthenia
395ᵀ	9ᵗʰ a.r.S Bro			Capt.	Sellars, Ronald G.	28	2 4/12	2/12	Neurasthenia
396ᵀ	5ᵗʰ Seaforths			2 Lt.	Macintosh J.	26	6 yrs	2 3/12	Neurasthenia
397ᵀ	R.W.F.	✝		2 Lt.	Sassoon, Siegfred	30	2 2/12	1 1/2	Neurasthenia
(25)	2ⁿᵈ R.S.			Major	Laidlaw John	29	8 4/12	1 yr	Neurasthenia
398ᵀ	1/4 Oxford & Bucks			Lt.	Proctor A.W.	34	2 8/12	2/12	Neurasthenia
399ᵀ	2/7 K. Liverpools			Lt.	Boak C.B.	32	2 6/12	5/12	Neurasthenia
400ᵀ	R.F.a. 166 Bde.			Lt.	Wadman C.R.	38	2 1/2	1 yr	Neurasthenia
(157ᵀ) }	13 Worcesters			2 Lt.	Hamm B.J.	21	1 4/12	3/12	Neurasthenia
401ᵀ	R.F.a.			Maj.	Farrant M.	31	10 7/12	2 11/12	Neurasthenia
402ᵀ	7 Yorks (London Regt.)			2 Lt.	Syre Chas.	19	1 5/12	7/12	Neurasthenia
403ᵀ	2/2 Lincolns			2 Lt.	Denby A.N.	33	2 10/12	1 3/12	Neurasthenia
404ᵀ	R.F.a.			Cap.	Shore C.M.S.	24	2 4/12	1 4/12	Neurasthenia
405ᵀ	2/10 London			2 Lt.	Morgan W.	19	2	6/12	Neurasthenia
406ᵀ	R.a.M.C.			Cap.	Ferguson R.L.	36	1 3/12	1 3/12	Neurasthenia
407ᵀ	A.S.C. (M.T.)			2 Lt.	Myers L.E.	23	2	7/12	Neurasthenia

Figure 33 The admission register for Craiglockhart Hospital (MH 106/1887)

FIELD SERVICE

Date of Admission		Date of Discharge			Date of Transfer				Number of days under treatment	Number or designation or ward in which treated	Religion	OBSERVATIONS
For original disease	By new disease super-vening	To Duty	By new disease super-vening	By Death	To		From					Number and page of case book to be quoted for all cases recorded in it. In transfers the designation of the hospital or sick convoy, to which or from which transferred, must be noted here, and any other facts bearing on the man's destination; also in moveable field hospitals the place where the admission, &c., took place should be indicated. Place of action to be noted in case of wounds and injuries received in action.
					Sick Convoy	Other Hospitals	Sick Convoy	Other Hospitals				
10 $\frac{7}{17}$		13 $\frac{4}{17}$						4th Lon.gen.116			C/E	
10 $\frac{7}{17}$		12 $\frac{8}{17}$						" 43			C/E	
10 $\frac{7}{17}$		11 $\frac{8}{17}$						" 32			C/E	
10 $\frac{7}{17}$		25 $\frac{8}{17}$						" 49			Pres.	
11 $\frac{7}{17}$		17 $\frac{7}{17}$ D.M.W.						Latchmere 68			C/E	
13 $\frac{7}{17}$		24 $\frac{12}{17}$ D.M.U.			1			York hill 164			Pres.	
13 $\frac{7}{17}$		10 $\frac{10}{17}$ D.M.W.						Dundee War H. 89			Pres.	
14 $\frac{7}{17}$		31 $\frac{10}{17}$ D.M.W.			18.7.17, Bros hill			4 Lon.gen. 104			C/E	
14 $\frac{7}{17}$		23 $\frac{4}{17}$ D.M.W.						" 162			3 Unit	
14 $\frac{7}{17}$		23 $\frac{10}{17}$						" 101			C/E	
14 $\frac{7}{17}$		11 $\frac{9}{17}$						2nd Western Gen. Manchester 59			C/E	
16 $\frac{7}{17}$		17 $\frac{7}{17}$. D.M						York hill 6			C/E	
14 $\frac{7}{17}$		10/18						4th Lon.gen. 184			C/E	
14 $\frac{7}{17}$		15 $\frac{4}{17}$ D.M.W.			24.7.17 Bros hill			" 104			C/E	
19 $\frac{7}{17}$		28 $\frac{8}{17}$						" Manchester 40			Pres.	
21 $\frac{7}{17}$		12 $\frac{9}{17}$						4th West.gen. 53			Pres.	From H.S.
23 $\frac{7}{17}$		26 $\frac{3}{18}$						Craig Leith 218. 23-10-17			Pres.	
23 $\frac{7}{17}$ Re-ad.		26 $\frac{11}{17}$ To Duty						1st Lon.gen. 124 22-3-17			C/E	From L. duty.
24-7-17.		7 $\frac{8}{17}$ H.S.						C.W.H. 14			C/E	from duty.
25 $\frac{7}{17}$		28 $\frac{7}{18}$ D.M.U						2nd Lon.gen. 218			C/E	
25 $\frac{7}{17}$		3 $\frac{1}{18}$. D.M.U						" 162			C/E	
25 $\frac{7}{17}$ Re-ad.		7 $\frac{4}{17}$			12-9. 31	30-10-17 Re-ad 31 "		" 105			C/E	
25 $\frac{7}{17}$		17 $\frac{10}{17}$ D.m.w.						" 84			C/E	
25 $\frac{7}{17}$		2 $\frac{10}{17}$			27-7-17. Coldstream M.			" 69			C/E	
25 $\frac{7}{17}$		18 $\frac{9}{17}$						" 55			C/E	
25 $\frac{7}{17}$		11 $\frac{9}{17}$						" 145			C/E	
25 $\frac{7}{17}$		4 $\frac{9}{17}$ To Duty						" 48			C/E	
25 $\frac{7}{17}$					Foulry aux. Hosp. East of Cornwall 1-11-17			" 105			C/E	
25 $\frac{7}{17}$		7 $\frac{9}{17}$			Roy. Lancs. Hosp. Blackpool			" 44			Cong.	
25 $\frac{7}{17}$		24 $\frac{9}{17}$						" 125			C/E	

Figure 34 A memorial plaque

Figure 35 A commemorative scroll

Information concerning officers killed during the Gallipoli operations can be found in *To What End Did They Die: Officers Who Died at Gallipoli*, R. W. Walker (1980).

A published list of all those killed on the first day of the Battle of the Somme, 1 July 1916, can be found in E. W. Bell (ed.) *Soldiers Killed on the First Day of the Somme* (1977), a copy of which is in the PRO Library.

Other published work available at the PRO includes the *Cross of Sacrifice* series by D. B. and S. B. Jarvis (1988–2000), which lists casualties by service, rank and in alphabetical order, giving date of death and place of commemoration.

The *National Roll of Honour 1914–1918* published in 14 volumes in the years after the war, covers the dead of a number of towns around the United Kingdom. Unusually the roll also includes those who survived the war. A copy of this work is available at the Imperial War Museum and at the Society of Genealogists, and is also due to be republished by Naval and Military Press in 2001.

Although not a roll as such, information regarding all of those officers of the rank of brigadier general or above who died or were wounded or captured, can be found in *Bloody Red Tabs* by F. Davies and G. Maddocks (1995).

13.9 Death certificates

Death certificates for service personnel who died during the war can be obtained from the Family Records Centre. See section **15.4**.

14 Records of the Dominion forces

14.1 Introduction

The records of service of members of the armed forces of the Dominions, Australia, Canada, New Zealand and South Africa are held by their respective national archives or appropriate government bodies. During the First World War the forces of these countries were considered by many to be the best troops in the British Army. However, many of the men who saw service in the forces of the Dominions were either British by birth or had British origins.

When requesting information from overseas please provide as much information about the individual as possible. Name, rank and number, if known, will really help.

14.2 Operational records

Although the Dominions kept their own operational records, many of which are preserved in their own archives, basic unit war diaries are preserved in the Public Record Office in the record series WO 95.

The unit war diaries held in the Canadian National Archives are more complete than those held in the PRO in as much as they have many of the personnel records which regiments were obliged to keep still with the diaries. It is therefore possible to find information concerning leave, sickness, promotions and postings. See section **14.5** for more information on the Canadian National Archives.

For more information about operational records, see **Chapter 7**.

14.3 Records of service: at the PRO

Although there are no generic collections of records of service for men of the Dominions, there are a number of files concerning British men who joined one of the Dominion forces in WO 364. These men are likely either to have joined the Dominions' forces in the UK, or to have been medically discharged and opted to remain in the UK rather than return to the Dominion they had served.

See **Chapter 3** for further information.

14.4 Records of service: Australia

Records of service of the Australian Imperial Forces (AIF) are held by the Australian National Archives in Canberra. It is possible to obtain copies from Australia and information concerning the records and a search service can be found on the Australian National Archives website, http://www.naa.gov.au The postal address to write to for these records is:

First World War Personnel Record Service
National Archives of Australia
PO Box 7425
Canberra Mail Centre ACT 2610
Australia

To access the information on the National Archives of Australia website, the following navigational information may help:

http://www.naa.gov.au
click on **The Collection**
click on **Defence**
click on **Conflicts**
find WW1 records of service

The Australian War Memorial (AWM), also in Canberra, has a number of very useful databases, some of which are on-line at http://www.awm.gov.au

Of the databases held by the AWM two are really useful. A Roll of Honour listing those members of the AIF who lost their lives and a Nominal Roll that lists those members of the AIF who went overseas can both be accessed by following this navigational advice:

http://www.awm.gov.au
click on **Australians at War**
click on **Biographical Databases**
find **Australians who served in WW1**
click on **Roll of Honour** or
click on **Nominal Roll**

14.5 Records of service: Canada

The records of service of the Canadian Expeditionary Force (CEF) are held by the National Archives of Canada in Ottawa. The first contingent of the CEF arrived in Britain in October 1914. A significant number of British men joined the CEF after it arrived in the UK simply because prior to 1916 entry into the British Army was still voluntary and the CEF offered better conditions and most importantly better pay.

Information concerning the records of the CEF can be obtained by writing to the following address:

Personnel Records Unit
National Archives of Canada
395 Wellington Street
Ottawa ON
K1A 0N3
Canada

Information about the CEF records is also available on-line at http://www. achives.ca

To access the information about the CEF records on-line the following navigational information may help:

http://www.achives.ca
click on **English**
under 'Research,' click on **Services**
click on **Military and Civilian Personnel Records**
click on **First World War CEF Database**
click on **Search Database**

The database can be searched using the fields, Surname, Given name(S) and Service Number(s).

The other large collection of military records held in Ottawa is the records of service of the Newfoundland Regiment. These records are in a separate collection as Newfoundland did not become part of Canada until 1947.

Amongst the other records held in Canada are what are known as 'Imperial Gratuities', which include land grants given to former members of the British Army, primarily Britons who wished to settle in Canada. The information contained in these records includes a detailed synopsis of their military careers.

14.6 Records of service: New Zealand

The military records of service of the New Zealand Expeditionary Force are held by the New Zealand Armed Forces at the following address:

Personnel Archives
Trentham Camp
Private Bag 905
Upper Hutt
New Zealand

Some brief information is available on the Internet on http://www.army.mil.nz. Click on Personnel Archives.

14.7 Records of service: South Africa

Surviving military records of service of men who saw service in the South African Forces during the First World War are held at the National Archives of South Africa. Searches can be carried out by contacting the following address:

Military Information Bureau
National Archives of South Africa
Private Bag X289
Pretoria 0001
South Africa

15 Records outside of the PRO

15.1 Introduction

The Public Record Office is not the only archive that preserves information about the First World War. Although the records of service and operational records are important, many other papers can be found at institutions around the United Kingdom.

15.2 Absent voters lists

Many people attempting to discover the record of service of an individual who saw service in the First World War have no idea as to their service details. Of all the records held outside of the PRO, the absent voters lists can provide that essential data.

By an Act of Parliament passed in February 1918, servicemen were allowed to register in order to be able to obtain a vote in their home constituency. These absent voter lists provide name, rank, number, unit and home address of each soldier registered.

The lists are not held by the PRO but are dispersed locally in the various archives of the counties and boroughs relevant to the areas the lists cover. The British Library has a small collection, but it is best to start at the County Record Office of the area where the soldier was registered to vote.

15.3 Newspapers

Of all the records produced during the First World War, national and local newspapers are a most underated source. Depending upon the unit, information about the personnel in it would quite often reach the press. Apart from casualty lists, which were published in *The Times*, information concerning local units, 'Pals' units for example, frequently appeared in local newspapers. Information about gallantry awards and promotions quite often appeared, as did photographs of many soldiers.

Copies of old local newspapers are often held by local libraries. The best collection of newspapers is held by the British Library at Colindale, see section **15.4.2**.

15.4 Other archives

Other archives where records concerning the First World War may be found include the following:

15.4.1 Imperial War Museum

The Imperial War Museum (IWM) has departments holding documents, printed books, photographs and oral history. Access to these records is by appointment.

For those with an interest in war memorials, the IWM holds the National Inventory of War Memorials.

The Imperial War Museum
Lambeth Road
London SE1 6HZ

Tel: 020 7416 5000
Website: http://www.iwm.org.uk

15.4.2 British Library

The British Library holds the records of the India Office including records of the Indian Army. Access is by reader's ticket, which can be obtained on the ground floor. The British Library also has a newspaper library at Colindale in north London.

The British Library
Oriental and India Office Collection
96 Euston Road
London NW1 2DR

Tel: 020 7412 7873
Website: http://www.bl.uk

The British Library Newspaper Library
Colindale Avenue
London NW9 5HE

Tel: 020 7412 7353

15.4.3 Commonwealth War Graves Commission

The Commonwealth War Graves Commission holds the cemetery registers and memorial registers for all of the graves and memorials it is responsible for. There is no public access. If you have access to the Internet, the CWGC Database is available on-line. Access is also available at the PRO.

The Commonwealth War Graves Commission
2 Marlow Road
Maidenhead
Berkshire SL6 7DX

Tel: 01628 634221
Website: http://www.cwgc.org.uk

15.4.4 National Army Museum

The National Army Museum holds a number of manuscript sources concerning the First World War. Access is by reader's ticket.

The National Army Museum
Royal Hospital Road
Chelsea
London SW3 4HT

Tel: 020 7730 0717
Website: http://www.national-army-museum.ac.uk

15.4.5 Family Records Centre

The ground floor of the Family Records Centre is run by the Office for National Statistics and holds the registers of births, marriages and deaths. The death records include separate registers for the war dead of the First World War. Copies of certificates can be obtained from the FRC or once you know the precise register details, by phone.

The Family Records Centre
1 Myddelton Street
London EC1R 1UW

Tel: 020 8392 5300
    0151 471 4816 certificate enquiries
Website: http://www.statistics.gov.uk

15.4.6 British Red Cross Museum and Archives

Access to the Red Cross Archives is by appointment.

British Red Cross Museum and Archives
9 Grosvenor Crescent
London SW1X 7EJ

Tel: 020 7201 5153
Website: http://www.redcross.org.uk

Bibliography

Abbott, P. E. and Tamplin, J. M. A., *British Gallantry Awards* (Nimrod Dix 1981)

The *Army List*

Battleground Europe series. Various authors (Leo Cooper 1994–2001)

Becke, A. F., *History of The Great War: Orders of Battle* (HMSO 1937–45)

Beckett, I. F. W. and Simpson, K., *A Nation in Arms: A Social Study of the British Army in the First World War* (Tom Donovan 1990)

Bell, E. W., ed., *Soldiers Killed on the First Day of the Somme* (1977)

Corrigan, G., *Sepoys in the Trenches: The Indian Corps on the Western Front 1914–1915* (Spellmount 1999)

Cox and Co., *List of Officers taken prisoner in the Various Theatres of War between August 1914 and November 1918*

Creagh, General O'Moore and Humphris, E. M., *The Distinguished Service Order 1886–1923* (Hayward 1988)

Davies, F. and Maddocks, G., *Bloody Red Tabs* (Leo Cooper 1995)

Dunn, J. C. *The War the Infantry Knew* (Cardinal 1989)

Farrington, A., *Guide to the Records of the India Office Military Department* (London 1982)

Holding, N., *World War I Army Ancestry* (FFHS 1997)

Holding, N., *More Sources of World War I Army Ancestry* (FFHS 1997)

The *Indian Army List*

James, E. A., *British Regiments 1914–1918* (Naval and Military Press 1993)

Jarvis, S. B. and D. B., *Cross of Sacrifice*, vols I–V (Roberts and Naval and Military Press 1988–2000)

Joslin, E. C., Litherland, A. R. and Simkin, B. T., *British Battles and Medals* (Spink 1988)

The *London Gazette*

McGregor, M., *Officers of the Durham Light Infantry* (McGregor 1989)

McInnes, I., *Meritorious Service Medal. The Immediate Awards 1916–1928* (Jade 1988)

McInnes, I., and Webb, J. V., *A Contemptible Little Flying Corps* (London Stamp Exchange 1991)

Middlebrook, M., *Your Country Needs You* (Leo Cooper 2000)

Officers Died in the Great War (HMSO 1922)

The Official History (HMSO various dates up to 1947)

Oram, G., *Death Sentences Passed by Military Courts of the British Army 1914–1920* (Francis Boutle 1998)

Oram, G. and Putkowski, J., *Officers Court Martialled by the British Army 1913–1924* (Francis Boutle 2001)

Putkowski, J. and Sykes, J., *Shot at Dawn* (Leo Cooper 1998)

Putkowski, J., *British Army Mutineers 1914–1922* (Francis Boutle 1999)

Simkins, P., *Kitchener's Army* (Manchester University Press 1990)

Soldiers Died in the Great War (HMSO 1922)

Spencer, W., *Air Force Records for Family Historians* (PRO 2000)

Spencer, W., *Records of the Militia and Volunteer Forces 1757–1945* (PRO 1998)

Statistics of British Military Effort (HMSO 1922)

Swinnerton, I., *Identifying Your World War I Soldier from Badges and Photographs* (FFHS 2001)

Walker, R. W., *To What End Did They Die: Officers Who Died at Gallipoli* (1980)

Walker, R. W., *Recipients of the Distinguished Conduct Medal 1914–1920* (Midland Medals 1980)

Westlake, R., *British Battalions on the Somme* (Leo Cooper 1994)

Westlake, R., *British Battalions at Gallipoli* (Leo Cooper 1996)

Westlake, R., *British Battalions in Belgium and France 1914* (Leo Cooper 1997)

Westlake, R., *British Battalions on the Western Front January – June 1915* (Leo Cooper 2000)

Westlake, R., *Kitchener's Army* (Spellmount 1998)

Whitehead, I. R., *Doctors in the Great War* (Leo Cooper 1999)

Wise, T., *Guide to Military Museum*, 9th edn (T. Wise 1999)

Index